Emerson's Evangelical Primer

by Joseph Emerson

Transcribed from the Armstrong edition of 1810 with certain words and phrases slightly revised by Dr. Byron Perrine, Editor, Our Christian Heritage Foundation, to more clearly communicate in the modern idiom.

To Which is Added

The Westminster Assembly's

Shorter Catechism

Our Christian Heritage Foundation

ISBN 10: 0615735274
ISBN-13: 978-0615735276

DEDICATION

This book is intended for use as a textbook for children preparing for confirmation, for pre-baptism classes, for children's Sunday School classes and home use, and, is dedicated to the use of all those entrusted with the responsibility and privilege of teaching those classes, assisting in the Lord's work of bringing their students to a more perfect understanding of the Gospel of Jesus Christ.

This is title one of the series
Historical Reprints by Our Christian Heritage Foundation

Also available:
The Religion that Shaped America, Dr. Byron Perrine, Editor

CONTENTS

Minor Doctrinal Catechism 7

Minor Historical Catechism 11

Assembly's Catechism With Notes and Proofs 47

Index for the Assembly's Catechism 80

Comments for Teachers 82

MINOR DOCTRINAL CATECHISM

Who made you? God.

What else did God make? He made the stones and hills, the brooks and trees, all living creatures, the sun, moon, and stars, and all other things.

Of what did God make all things? Of nothing, Heb. 11:3.

For whom did God make all things? For himself.

How long has God lived? Always without beginning.

Where is God? Everywhere.

When does God see you? By day and by night; he sees me, when I do wrong, and always sees me.

What does God know? He knows all things. If I tell a lie, he knows it; if I speak an idle or wicked word, he hears it. He knows every word that I speak, and every thought that I think.

What has God done for you? He has made me, and kept me alive; he has given me food to eat, and clothes to wear, and all other blessings, that I have enjoyed.

What is the greatest thing that God has ever done for you and the rest of mankind? He gave his Son Jesus Christ, to die for us, Heb. 2:9.

What need was there, that Christ should die for

you? To atone for my sins.

How have you sinned? I have not faithfully remembered by Creator, to love him with all my heart, to pray to him, and to keep his holy Sabbath; and I have done many other things, which he has forbidden.

What is the general character of the natural heart? It is enmity against God; it is deceitful above all things, and desperately wicked, Jer. 17:9.

What is meant by the natural heart? It is a heart, that has not been renewed by the Holy Spirit, John 3:6.

What if Christ had not died for you and others? We must have been punished for all our sins, as we deserve,

What do you deserve? I deserve everlasting destruction in hell.

Will Christ save you from hell? If I repent of my sins, and believe in him, he will save me from hell, and raise me to heaven.

Can Christ raise you to heaven? He can; for he is the mighty God, the everlasting Father, Is. 9:6.

What kind of a place is heaven? It is a most happy place. There is no night there; neither is there any sin, nor death, nor sickness, nor pain, nor sorrow, Rev. 7:16, 17.

Why is there no night there? Because Christ, the Sun of righteousness, is there, and he is the light of heaven.

If you go to heaven, what company shall you there enjoy? I shall enjoy the company of the holy angels, glorified saints, and of Christ himself.

How are glorified saints employed? There are employed in loving one another, in loving the angels, and in uniting their hearts and voices in loving, adoring, and praising God and the Redeemer.

How long will their blessed employments continue? Forever and ever.

If you were carried to heaven, should you be happy there? I could not be happy even in heaven without being born again, and having a new heart.

Why could you not be happy in heaven without being born again? I should not love Christ, nor angels, nor saints; and could not join in the heavenly employments.

What proves a change of heart? Repentance toward God and faith in Jesus Christ.

What is true repentance toward God? It is to abhor sin, as committed against him; to abhor myself for sin, and to reform.

What is false repentance? It is sorrow, arising from fear of punishment, without hating sin.

What is true faith in Jesus Christ? It is humbly receiving him as my Teacher, Lord, and Savior, giving myself to him, and trusting in him alone for salvation.

What is false faith? It is holding the truths of the gospel in unrighteousness; or believing that Jesus was the Son of God, without loving him. It is such a faith as the devils have.

What reasons have you to trust in Christ alone for salvation? There is salvation in no other. He is mighty to save. Those who come to him he will in no wise cast out, but will give them eternal life.

Shall you not die, if you trust in Christ? I shall, for all men must die.

What will become of your body after you die? It will return to dust, and so continue till the last day.

What will be done at the last day? The bodies of all mankind will be raised, the earth will be burnt up, and the final judgment will take place.

Who will be the Judge? Christ, Rom. 14:10.

In what manner will he come to judgment? He will be revealed from heaven with his mighty angels in flaming fire.

Who must stand before the judgment seat of Christ? All mankind, Mat. 25:32.

For what must you then give account to Christ? For all my actions, words, and thoughts.

What will Christ then say to the righteous? Come, ye blessed of my Father, inherit the kingdom, prepared for you from the foundation of the world, Mat. 25:34.

What will Christ then say to the wicked? Depart from me, ye cursed, into everlasting fire, prepared for the devil and his angels, Mat. 25:41.

What will be your condition in hell, if you die in your sins? I shall be dreadfully tormented.

What company will be there? There will be legions of devils, and multitudes of sinners of the human race.

Will company afford you any comfort in hell, if you go to that place of torment? It will not, but will probably increase my woes.

If you should go to hell, how long must you continue there? Forever and ever; as long as God shall exist. Mat. 25:46.

Why do you not immediately repent, and flee from the wrath to come? I can offer no good excuse for not repenting.

If you should die in your sins, and God should make you miserable, should you miserable, should you have any reason to complain of him? Not the least. I must be speechless, Mat. 22:12.

The Lord's Prayer. Our Father, etc. Mat. 6:9-13

MINOR HISTORICAL CATECHISM

Lesson 1.

Who was the first man? Adam.

Who was the first woman? Eve.

Who tempted Adam to sin? Eve.

Who tempted Eve? The serpent.

Who is the serpent? Satan, Rev. 20:2.

Who was to bruise the serpent's head? The Seed of the woman, Gen 3:15.

Who is the Seed of the woman? Christ

Who murdered Abel? Cain, Gen 4:8.

What became of Enoch? He was carried to heaven without dying, Heb. 11:5.

Who was the oldest man? Methuselah.

Who walked with God, when the earth was filled with violence? Noah.

How did he manifest his faith? By building an ark to save himself and his family from the flood.

Lesson 2.

Who is the father of believers? Abraham, Rom. 4:11.

Who was his first wife ? Sarah.

How did Abraham manifest his faith? By leaving his country, and offering up his son Isaac at God's command. Heb. 11:8, 17.

What righteous man dwelt in Sodom? Lot.

After Lot was carried away captive, by whom was he delivered? By Abraham, Gen. 14:14-16.

Who blessed Abraham, after he had delivered Lot? Melchizedek, Gen. 14:19.

How were Sodom and Gomorrah destroyed? By a storm of brimstone and fire, Gen. 19: 24,25.

Why were they destroyed? For the great wickedness of their inhabitants, Gen. 13:13.

Lesson 3.

Who was Abraham's child of promise? Isaac, Gal. 4:28, 29.

Who was Isaac's wife? Rebekah, Gen. 24: 67.

Who were Isaac's sons? Esau and Jacob, Gen. 25:21-26.

Who sold his birthright? Esau.

Who obtained the blessing, that was intended for his brother? Jacob, Gen. 27:35.

Who were Jacob's wives? Leah and Rachel.

Who was their father? Laban, Gen. 29.

Which of the wives did Jacob love most? Rachel.

Why was Jacob's name changed to Israel? Because he prayed, till he obtained a blessing.

How many sons had Jacob? Twelve, Gen. 35:22.

Which of them wickedly slew the Shechemites?
Simeon and Levi.

Which of his sons did Jacob love most? Joseph.

What did Jacob give him as a token of special love?
A coat of many colors.

How did Joseph's brothers feel toward him at that time? They hated him, Gen. 37:3, 4.

Why did Joseph go to Shechem? To seek his brothers.

Where did he find them? At Dothan.

What did they say, when they saw him? Behold this dreamer is coming.

How did they then treat him? They stripped him of his coat of many colors, cast him into a pit, and then sold him to a company of Ishmaelites, Gen. 37.

How was Jacob affected by the loss of Joseph? His affliction was so great, that he refused to be comforted, Gen. 37:31-35.

Lesson 4.

What did the Ishmaelites do with Joseph? They carried him into Egypt, and sold him to Potiphar, an officer of Pharaoh, Gen. 37:36.

How did Potiphar treat Joseph? He made him overseer over his house, Gen. 39:4.

What induced Potiphar to put Joseph into prison?
The false and cruel accusation of Potiphar's wife.

How did the keeper of the prison treat Joseph? He committed all the prisoners to his care.

For whom did Joseph interpret dreams in prison?
The chief butler and chief baker of Pharaoh, Gen. 40.

What other dreams did he interpret? Pharaoh's, Gen. 41.

To what did Pharaoh's dreams relate? Seven years of plenty, and seven years of amine.

How did Pharaoh reward Joseph? By making him ruler over Egypt.

For what did Joseph's brothers first go into Egypt? To buy grain.

How did he treat them at that time? Roughly.

When was he made known to them? At their second going into Egypt.

What did Joseph do for his father and his father's family? He sent for them, to come down into Egypt and nourished them there, Gen. 45 and 46.

In what part of Egypt did they settle? In Goshen, Gen. 47:6.

Lesson 5.

How did the Egyptians treat the children of Israel? Very kindly for a number of years, and afterwards very cruelly.

What wicked command did Pharaoh give his people? He commanded them to cast the infant sons of Israel into a river.

Who was hid three months by his mother, that he might not be cast into the river? Moses.

What did she then do with him? She put him into a little ark or basket, and placed it by the side of the river among the reeds, Ex. 2:3.

Who found him? Pharaoh's daughters, Ex. 2:10.

How did she treat him? She adopted him for her son, Acts 7:21.

To whom did she commit him for nursing? To his mother.

In what did he become learned? In all the wisdom

of the Egyptians.

Why did he refuse to be called the son of Pharaoh's daughter? He chose rather to suffer affliction with the people of God, than to enjoy the pleasures of sin for a season, Heb.11:25.

Why did Moses slay an Egyptian? For smiting one of the Hebrews.

Who were the Hebrews? The Israelites.

Why was not Moses slain for killing the Egyptian? He fled into Midian, Ex. 2:15.

Whose flock did he keep in Midian? Jethro's, Ex. 3:1.

Whom did Moses marry? Zipporah, Jethro's daughter.

Lesson 6.

How did God first appear to Moses? In a burning bush.

Why did God then appear to Moses? To send him into Egypt, to deliver the Hebrews from bondage, Ex. 3:10.

Whom did God send out of Egypt, to meet Moses, in order to go with him into Egypt, and assist him in delivering the Hebrews? Aaron, his elder brother, Ex. 4.

How many plagues were sent upon the Egyptians, before Pharaoh would let Israel go? Ten

What was the last and most dreadful of these plagues? Slaying all the first born of the Egyptians, Ex. 11.

What was instituted to commemorate the preservation of Israel from that plague? The Passover, Ex. 12.

Why was it so called? Because, when the Lord

smote the Egyptians, he passed over the Israelites without hurting them, Ex. 12:12, 13.

What did Pharaoh do, when he found the Israelites were gone out of Goshen? He pursued them with this army.

How did the Israelites escape the Egyptians? They went through the Red Sea on dry ground.

What became of the Egyptians? In attempting to follow the Israelites they were drowned in the Red Sea, Ex. 14.

How did the Israelites acknowledge their deliverance from the Egyptians? In a song of praise to God, Ex. 15.

Lesson 7.

Where was the law given? At Mount Sinai.

How were the ten commandments given? God spoke them in a loud voice, so that all Israel could hear, Ex. 19:9, 19 and 20:1.

Upon what did God write them? Upon two tablets of stone. Ex. 24:12.

What great sin did the Israelites commit, while Moses was receiving the law on the mountain with God? They made and worshipped a golden calf, Ex. 32.

When Moses saw the calf and the people dancing round it, what did he do with the two tables of stone? He cast them down and broke them.

How were they replaced? Moses prepared two others; and God wrote the commandments upon them, Ex. 34.

Where were they afterwards kept? In an ark or chest made for the purpose.

Lesson 8.

Who was the first Levitical priest? Aaron.

From whom did the other Levitical priests descend? From Aaron.

Who were struck dead for offering strange fire? Nadab and Abihu, sons of Aaron, Lev. 10.

What is meant by strange fire? That which God had not commanded.

How many men were sent from Kadeshbarnea to spy out Canaan? Twelve, one of each tribe, Num. 13.

Who of them brought back a good report of the land? Caleb and Joshua, Num. 14:6-7.

How were they rewarded? They were permitted to enter Canaan, Num. 14:24, 30.

What report did the other ten spies bring back? A very evil report; they slandered the land.

What judgment befell them? They died of the plague.

What Israelites murmured against God in the wilderness? Most of those, who were above 20 years old when they came out of Egypt.

What became of them? They were destroyed in the wilderness, Num. 26:65.

What was the character of those who were under 20 years old, when they came out of Egypt? They were generally pious, Jer. 2:2-3. Heb. 3:16.

Lesson 9.

What was done to the man, who gathered sticks on the Sabbath? He was stoned to death, Num. 15:36.

Who were destroyed for rebelling against Moses and Aaron? Korah and his company, Num. 16.

How were they destroyed? Some were swallowed up by the earth; and some were slain by fire from the Lord.

What was done to the son of Shelomith for cursing and blasphemy? He was stoned to death, Lev. 24:10-16, 23.

Who first refused to let Israel pass through his land? The king of Edom, Num. 20:14-21.

Where did Aaron die? On Mount Hor, Num. 20.

Who lifted up the brazen serpent in the wilderness? Moses, Num. 21.

For what purpose? That those, who should be bitten by serpents, might look upon it and live, Num. 21.

What did the brazen serpent represent? Christ.

Who besides the king of Edom refused to let Israel pass through his land? Sihon, king of the Amorites, Num. 21:23.

How did they punish him? They slew him.

Who came out against Israel at Edrei? Og, king of Bashan.

What became of him and his people? They were smitten by the Israelites, Num. 21:33-35.

Lesson 10.

Where was the last encampment of Israel, before they entered Canaan? On the plains of Moab, a few miles east of the river Jordan.

Who were greatly terrified at the time on account of Israel? The Moabites, Num. 22:3.

Who was king of Moab at that time? Balak.

For whom did he send, to come and curse Israel? Balaam.

Why did Balaam wish to go and curse Israel? He loved the wages of unrighteousness, 2 Pet. 2:15.

By what was he rebuked for his iniquity? By the beast on which he rode, miraculously speaking, 2 Pet. 2:16.

Why did not Balaam curse Israel? The Lord would not permit him to do it.

What great injury did Balaam do to Israel? He taught Balak to seduce them to commit idolatry and fornication, Rev. 2:14.

How many of the Israelites died of the plague for yielding to the temptation? 24 thousand.

What became of Balaam? He was slain by the Israelites, Num. 31:8.

Lesson 11.

How long were the Israelites in the wilderness? 40 years.

How did God lead them? By a pillar, that appeared like a cloud by day, and like fire by night, Ex. 13:21.

What was their principal food? Manna, Ex. 16:15.

Where did they find it? On the ground.

How did it come to be there? God produced it miraculously.

How often did they gather it? Every morning except the Sabbath.

How did the Israelites behave in the wilderness? A great part of them often rebelled against God, Deut. 9.

For what purpose did Moses ascend mount Nebo? To view Canaan, and die, Deut. 34.

Why was he not permitted to enter Canaan? Because on a certain occasion he rebelled against the Lord,
Num. 27:14.

Lesson 12.

Who was the leader of Israel after the death of Moses? Joshua.

Through what river did they pass on dry ground? The river Jordan, Josh. 3:16-17.

On what occasion did the walls of Jericho fall down? At the shouting of the Israelites, after the walls had been compassed 7 days, Heb. 11:30.

Who of the people of Jericho were preserved alive? Rahab and her father's family.

Who was slain for taking of the accursed thing, and for dissembling? Achan, Josh. 7.

Who deceived the Israelites, by pretending that they lived at a very great distance? The Gibeonites, Josh. 9.

At whose word did the sun and moon stand still? Joshua's, Josh. 10.

How long did Israel continue to serve the Lord, after entering Canaan? All the days of Joshua and of the elders who had seen the great works of the Lord, which he had done for Israel, Judg. 2:7.

What was the character of the next generation? They were very wicked, Judg. 2:10.

How did the Lord punish them? He delivered them into the hand of plunderers, Judg. 2:14.

What were those persons called, who were raised up, to deliver Israel? Judges.

Lesson 13.

Who delivered Israel from Cushan-Rishathaim, king of Mesopotamia? Othniel, Judg. 3:9.

Who delivered them from Eglon, king of Moab? Ehud, Judg. 3:15.

Who killed 600 Philistines with an ox goad?

Shamgar, Judg. 3:31.

Who drove a nail through the head of Sisera? Jael, the wife of Heber the Kenite, Judg. 4:21.

Who delivered Israel from the Midianites? Gideon, Judg. 7.

Who assisted him? 300 men, with trumpets, pitchers, and lamps.

Who killed 70 sons of Gideon? Abimelech, their wicked brother.

Who made Abimelech king? The men of Shechem and the house of Millo, Judg. 9:6.

What became of Abimelech? He was slain.

Who delivered Israel from the Ammonites? Jephthah, Judg. 11.

Who was the strongest man? Samson.

How many Philistines did he kill with the jaw bone? 1000, Judg. 15:15.

How did he become weak? By having his hair shaved off, Judg. 16:19.

Who enticed him to tell wherein his great strength lay? Delilah.

How did the Philistines treat him then? They put out his eyes, and cast him into prison.

When they were assembled to worship Dagon, for what purpose did they send for Samson? To make sport.

What did Samson do to the Philistines, after they had sent for him? He pulled down the house, in which great multitudes were assembled, and thus killed them, Judg. 16.

Who was greatly distressed for the loss of his gods? Micah, Judg. 18.

Lesson 14.

How did Samuel behave, when he was a child? He served the Lord, 1 Sam. 2:18.

With whom did he then live? With Eli, the priest and judge of Israel.

By whom was the ark of God taken captive? By the Philistines.

How was Eli affected by this? He fell backward and died, 1 Sam. 4:18.

Where did the Philistines place the ark? In the house of Dagon, their idol, 1 Sam. 5:2.

What then happened to Dagon? He fell down before the ark, and was broken, that it might be known that he was no god.

Why did the Philistines restore the ark to Israel? Because judgments were sent upon them.

Who were smitten for looking into the ark? A number of the Bethshemites.

When Samuel was old, whom did he make judges? His sons, 1 Sam. 8.

How did they behave? Very wickedly.

What did the people wickedly request of Samuel? A king, 1 Sam. 8.

Why did they wish for a king? That in that respect they might be like other nations.

Whom did Samuel anoint for their first king? Saul, 1 Sam. 9.

How did Saul behave after he was made king? Well at first, and then wickedly.

Whom did he condemn to die for tasting a little honey? His son Jonathan, 1 Sam. 14:44.

Who rescued Jonathan from Saul? The people.

What nation was Saul commanded to destroy? The

Amalekites.

Whom of them did he spare? Agag, their king.

What did Samuel do to Agag? He hewed him in pieces, 1 Sam. 15.

Why did the Lord reject Saul from being king? Because he rejected the Lord.

Whom did Samuel anoint for the next king? David, 1 Sam. 16.

For what purpose did David play upon a harp before Saul? To drive away an evil spirit, that troubled Saul, 1 Sam. 16.

Lesson 15.

Who defied the armies of the living God? Goliath, a Philistine, 1 Sam. 17.

Who slew him? David.

How? Slung a stone into his forehead, and then cut off his head.

Who often attempted to kill David? Saul.

Who loved David as his own soul? Jonathan.

Who was David's first wife? Michal, Saul's daughter.

How many times did David flee to Gath for fear of Saul? Twice.

Who killed 85 priests of the Lord in a day? Doeg, the Edomite, 1 Sam. 22:18.

What did Saul do, when he was greatly distressed on account of the Philistines? He consulted a woman, who had a familiar spirit at Endor.

Why did the lords of the Philistines prevent David's going to war against Israel? They feared he would turn against the Philistines in battle, 1 Sam. 29.

Where did Saul and Jonathan die? On Mount

Gilboa, in battle with the Philistines, 1 Sam 31.

How did David behave on hearing of the death of Saul and Jonathan? He wept, and lamented over them, 2 Sam. 1:11, 12, 17.

Lesson 16.

Where was David made king of Judah? At Hebron, 2 Sam. 2.

Who was made king over the rest of Israel at that time? Ishbosheth, son of Saul.

By whom? By Abner.

Why did Joab murder Abner? Because Abner had killed Asahel, Joab's brother, 2 Sam. 3:27.

Who murdered Ishbosheth? Rechab and Baanah, 2 Sam. 4.

How did David punish them? He caused them to be put to death, 2 Sam. 4.

How long did David reign over Judah at Hebron? Seven years and six months, 2 Sam. 5:5.

Over whom did he then reign? Over all Israel at Jerusalem.

Lesson 17.

Why was Uzzah slain? For taking hold of the ark.

Why was David forbidden to build a house for the Lord? Because he had been a great warrior (and shed much blood), 1 Chron. 22:8.

Who reproved David for his great wickedness in the case of Uriah? Nathan, 2 Sam. 12.

In what psalm has David expressed his deep repentance for that sin? In the fifty-first.

What will be the portion of such as imitate David's sins without imitating his repentance? They will have their part in the lake, that burns with fire and brimstone.

Who killed Amnon? Absalom, 2 Sam. 13.

Whose sons were Amnon and Absalom? David's.

To whom did Absalom flee? To his grandfather Talmai, king of Geshur.

By whose counsel was Absalom brought back? Joab's, 2 Sam. 14.

For what was Absalom greatly praised? For his beauty, 2 Sam. 14:25.

How did Absalom steal away the hearts of the people? By fair words and pretended affection.

What was his conduct towards David afterwards? He rebelled against him.

When David was fleeing from Absalom, who cursed him? Shimei, 2 Sam. 16:3.

Lesson 18.

After Absalom had taken possession of Jerusalem, what was the counsel of Ahithophel? To pursue David immediately, 2 Sam. 17.

What was the counsel of Hushai? Togather all Israel together, and to pursue David with their whole force.

Which was followed? The counsel of Hushai.

What did Ahithophel do, when he found his counsel was rejected? He hung himself, 2 Sam 17:23.

What became of Absalom? As he rode under an oak, when fleeing in battle, his head was caught by the branches, where he hung, til Joab thrust him through with three darts, 2 Sam. 18.

How did David bear the news of Absalom's death? He mourned and wept exceedingly.

How did Joab treat Amasa? He treacherously

murdered him, 2 Sam. 20.

Lesson 19.

Who excited the second rebellion against David?
Sheba, 2 Sam. 20.

What became of Sheba? He was slain.

*What judgment was sent upon Israel for David's
numbering the people?* A dreadful pestilence, 2 Sam.
24.

How many people died of that pestilence? 70
thousand.

*When David was old, who attempted to reign in his
stead?* Adonijah, 1 Kings 1:5.

Whom did the Lord appoint, to succeed David?
Solomon, 1 Chron. 22:9-10.

What became of Adonijah? He was slain by order of
Solomon.

Lesson 20.

For what was Solomon distinguished? For wisdom
and riches, 2 Chron.1:12.

When did Solomon build the temple? About 1000
years before the birth of Christ.

*Who came from a far country, to prove Solomon's
wisdom?* The queen of Sheba, 2 Chron. 9.

*What was the general character of Solomon's
reign?* Peaceful and prosperous, 1 Chron. 22:9.

*What was the immediate consequence of his loving
many strange women?* His heart was turned to idolatry.

What is meant by strange women? Those who were
not Israelites.

*What judgments did God denounce against
Solomon for his aggravated sins?* That the kingdom

should be taken from him, and given to his servant, 1 Kings 11:11.

What merciful conditions were added to this threatening? That God would not tear away the kingdom in Solomon's days, and that he would not tear away the whole kingdom.

Lesson 21.

Who succeeded Solomon? Rehoboam, his son.

Where did Israel assemble to make Rehoboam king? At Shechem.

What did they request of him? That he would lighten the burdens, which they had borne in the days of Solomon.

How did Rehoboam answer them? Very roughly, 1 Kings 12:13.

What was the effect of this rough treatment? Ten tribes rebelled against Rehoboam.

What tribes adhered to Rehoboam? Judah and Benjamin, generally called Judah, 1 Kings 12:17.

Whom did Rehoboam send to the revolted tribes? Hadoram.

How did they treat Hadoram? They killed him, 1 Chron. 10:18.

What did Rehoboam then do, to bring Israel under him? He raised an army, to fight against them, 1 Kings 12:21.

Why did he not proceed against them? The Lord forbade him.

Lesson 22.

Who was made king of the ten tribes? Jeroboam, the son of Nebat.

How did he behave? Very wickedly indeed. He

made Israel to sin.

How did he make Israel to sin? By setting up two golden calves, and persuading the people to worship them.

Where were these golden calves placed? One at Dan, and the other at Bethel, 1 Kings 12:29.

Who cried out against Jeroboam's altar at Bethel? A prophet from Judah, 1 Kings 13: 1-2.

What happened to that prophet for disobeying the Lord? He was slain by a lion.

Who was a pious child of Jeroboam? Abijah.

What was the character of Rehoboam? He was a wicked man, 2 Chron. 12:1.

Lesson 23.

Why did Asa remove Maachah from being a queen? Because she made an idol in a grove.

What was the character of Ahab? He was more wicked than any king of Israel before him.

Who stirred him up to do wickedly? Jezebel, his wife, 1 Kings 21:25.

Who has been celebrated for fervent, effectual prayer? Elijah, James 5.

How was Elijah fed at the brook Cherith? By ravens, 1 Kings 17:6.

Whom did Elijah raise to life? The son of a woman of Sarepta, 1 Kings 17:22.

When Jezebel killed the Lord's prophets, who hid and fed a hundred of them? Obadiah, 1 Kings 18:4.

How many prophets of Baal did Elijah kill? 450.

Who tried to kill him for this? Jezebel, 1 Kings 19.

To where did Elijah flee from Jezebel? To Mount Horeb, 1 Kings 19:8.

Lesson 24.

Who besieged Samaria with 32 kings assisting him?
Benhadad, king of Syria, 1 Kings 20

Did he succeed? He was twice beaten by Israel with
great slaughter.

*What did the Lord say to Ahab for sparing
Benhadad?* Thy life shall go for his life, and thy people
for his people.

Whose vineyard did Ahab covet? Naboth's.

How did Jezebel obtain it for Ahab? By causing
Naboth to be killed, 1 Kings 21.

What became of Ahab? In battle with the Syrians at
Ramoth Gilead, he was mortally wounded by a man who
drew a bow at random, 1 Kings 22:34-35.

What became of Jezebel? She was thrown down
from a window, and devoured by dogs, 2 Kings 9:33-36.

*What happened to the two first companies of 50
men, that Ahaziah sent to take Elijah?* They were
consumed by fire from heaven.

How was Elijah carried to heaven? In a chariot of
fire by a whirlwind.

*What became of the 42 wicked youths, that mocked
Elisha?* They were torn in pieces by two bears, 2 Kings
2:24.

Lesson 25.

Whom did Elisha raise to life? The son of a
Shunammite, 2 Kings 4.

*Who was cleansed of his leprosy by washing in
Jordan?* Naaman, the Syrian, 2 Kings 5.

*What reason is assigned for the great wickedness of
Jehoram, king of Judah?* The daughter of Ahab was his

wife.

What reason is assigned for the wickedness of Ahaziah? His mother was his counselor to do wickedly, 2 Chron. 22:3.

What was the character of Jehu, king of Israel? Though he pretended great zeal for the Lord, he was an idolater, 2 King 10.

Lesson 26.

Who concealed Joash from Athaliah, when she slew the seed royal of Judah? Jehosheba his aunt.

Who reigned over Judah during his concealment? Athaliah.

What revolution then took place? Joash was made king, and Athaliah was slain, 2 Kings 11.

How was Zechariah treated for his faithfulness to Joash? He was slain.

What effect had great prosperity upon Uzziah? It caused his heart to be lifted up, to his destruction, 2 Chron. 26:16.

What judgment befell him for attempting to burn incense in the temple? He was smitten with leprosy.

Why is Isaiah sometimes called the evangelical prophet? Because he prophesied so much concerning Christ and his kingdom.

When did he begin to prophesy? In the latter part of Uzziah's reign, about 760 years before the coming of Christ.

Who began to prophesy a little before Isaiah? Jonah, Joel, Amos, and Hosea.

Lesson 27.

What was the general character of the kings of

Israel? They were all wicked, and all idolaters except perhaps Hoshea, the last king.

Was not he an idolater? It is probable, but no certain, that he was, 2 Kings 17.

How did God reprove Israel for their idolatry and wickedness? By his judgments and also by his prophets, particularly Elijah and Elisha.

How did Go punish Israel for the sins? After sending many judgments upon them, he gave them up into the hand of the Assyrians.

What king of Assyria carried them captive? Shalmaneser, 2 Kings 17.

When were they carried captive? In the sixth year of Hezekiah, king of Judah, about 721 years before the coming of Christ.

Lesson 28.

What was the general character of the kings of Judah? About half of them were idolaters, and most of the rest were good men.

Who of them were great reformers? Asa, Hezekiah, and Josiah.

How long did they reign? Asa reigned 41 years, Hezekiah 29, and Josiah 31.

What kings of Judah were most noted for wickedness? Ahaz and Manasseh.

How did Ahaz behave under great judgments? He sinned more and more.

Who invited all Israel to attend the Passover at Jerusalem? Hezekiah, 2 Chron. 30.

What king of Assyria came up against Judah in the days of Hezekiah? Sennacherib, 2 Kings 18.

How many Assyrians were slain by an angel in one

night? 185 thousand, 2 Kings 19:35.

What became of Sennacherib? He was soon after slain by two of his sons while he was worshipping his idol.

Lesson 29.

How did God punish Manasseh for his sins? He delivered him into the hand of the Assyrians, who bound him and carried him to Babylon.

What was his conduct at Babylon? He sought the Lord his God, and humbled himself greatly.

How did God punish Judah for their sins? After visiting them with many judgments, he gave them up into the hand of Nebuchadnezzar, who carried them captive to Babylon, 2 Chron. 36.

What kings did he carry to Babylon? Jehoiachin and Zedekiah.

At how many times were the people of Judah carried captive? Principally at three times.

Who burnt the temple, and destroyed Jerusalem? Nebuzaradan, a principal officer of Nebuchadnezzar, 2 Kings 25.

Lesson 30.

Why is Jeremiah sometimes called the weeping prophet? Because he wept so much for the sins and miseries of his nation.

Who prophesied in the days of Jeremiah? Habakkuk, Zephaniah, and Ezekiel.

Who prophesied in the time of the Babylonian captivity? Jeremiah, Ezekiel, Obadiah, and Daniel.

Where did Ezekiel prophesy? In Chaldea, not far

from Babylon.

Where did Daniel prophesy? At Babylon.

Who was governor of the remnant of the Jews, that were left in Judea after the Babylonian captivity? Gedaliah, Jer. 40.

Who treacherously murdered Gedaliah? Ishmael, Jer. 41.

What became of the remnant of the Jews? Contrary to the divine command, they went down into Egypt, where most of them for abominable idolatries were delivered into the hand of Nebuchadnezzar, and slain, Jer. 42 & 43 & 44.

Lesson 31.

Who interpreted Nebuchadnezzar's dreams? Daniel, Dan. 2 & 4.

What was the character of Daniel? He was a man of uncommon wisdom and piety.

Who refused to worship the golden image, which Nebuchadnezzar set up? Shadrach, Meshach, and Abednego.

What was done to them? They were cast into a burning, fiery furnace, Dan. 3:21.

Why did not the fire hurt them? God delivered them from its power.

How was Nebuchadnezzar punished for his pride? He was deprived of his reason, and driven from among men for 7 years, Dan. 4.

Who was so terrified that his knees knocked together? Belshazzar, Dan. 5:6.

By whom was Babylon taken in the days of Daniel? By Darius the Mede.

Why was Daniel cast into a den of lions? For praying to God, Dan. 6.

Why did not the lions hurt him? God shut their mouths.

Lesson 32.

How long did the Babylonian captivity continue? 70 years, 2 Ch. 36:21.

Who gave the Jews permission to return to Canaan? Cyrus, Ezra 1.

Who built the second temple? Zerubbabel, called also Sheshbazzar.

Who opposed, and hindered the work? Rehum, Shimshai, and the rest of the Samaritans.

Who married Esther? Ahasuerus, king of Persia.

Who was greatly promoted by Ahasuerus? Haman, Esth. 3:1.

Who refused to bow to Haman? Mordecai.

What revenge did Haman seek? He sought to destroy all the Jews in the kingdom of Ahasuerus, Esth. 3:6.

How were they saved from destruction? By means of Esther's intercession to Ahasuerus.

How was Haman punished? He was hanged upon the gallows, that he had prepared for Mordecai, Esth. 7:10.

Who rebuilt the wall of Jerusalem? Nehemiah.

Who greatly assisted him in the work? Artaxerxes, the king of Persia, Neh. 2.

Who greatly opposed the work? Sanballat, Tobiah, and Geshem, Neh. 4.

How did they feel, when the work was finished?

Much cast down in their own eyes, Neh. 4:10.

Lesson 33.

Who came into the world to save sinners? Jesus Christ, 1 Tim. 1:15.

Who spoke of him before he was born? The prophets and the angel Gabriel.

Who was the mother of Jesus? Mary.

Who was his immediate father? Not man, but God.

Who was Mary's husband and the reputed father of Jesus? Joseph.

Where was Christ born? In a stable at Bethlehem, Luke 2.

Who was sent in the spirit and power of Elijah, to prepare the way before Christ? John the Baptist, Luke 1:17.

Why was John called the Baptist? Because he was sent to baptize.

Lesson 34.

Who were directed by a star, to find Christ? Wise men from the east.

Who sought to kill the infant Jesus? Herod.

How was Jesus delivered from Herod? By being carried into Egypt, and kept there until Herod was dead, Mat. 2.

Where was Jesus brought up? At Nazareth, Luke 4:16.

How old was Jesus, when he went up to Jerusalem, and conversed with the doctors in the temple? 12 years, Luke 2:42.

How old was he, when he was baptized by John? About 30 years, Luke 3:23.

Who tempted Christ in the wilderness? Satan. Mat. 4; Luke 4.

How long? 40 days.

How did Christ describe the virtues of John the Baptist? He said he was a burning and a shining light, a prophet and much more than a prophet.

Whom did John reprove for having his brother's wife? Herod, a son of the Herod who destroyed the infants of Bethlehem. Mat. 14.

How did Herod treat John? He imprisoned him, and afterwards killed him.

Lesson 35.

Where did Jesus perform his first miracle? In Cana of Galilee, John 2:11.

Where did Jesus make it his home, after he began his public ministry? At Capernaum, Mat. 4:13.

Where did Jesus preach? In all the cities and villages of Galilee, and in other parts of the land of Israel.

On what occasions did he go to Jerusalem? On occasion of the Passover, and some other feasts of the Jews.

What ruler of the Jews conversed with Jesus by night? Nicodemus, John 3.

Who said that Jesus told her all things that ever she did? A woman of Samaria, John 4.

How did the people of Nazareth treat Jesus for his faithful preaching? They attempted to kill him, Luke 4:29.

How many disciples did Christ choose to be with him, and ordain to be apostles? Twelve.

Why did Christ pronounce woes on those cities, in which most of his mighty works were done? Because they did not repent, Mat. 11:20.

What cities in particular did he thus upbraid?
Chorazin, Bethsaida, and Capernaum.

Whom did Christ particularly warn of the danger of blasphemy against the Holy Spirit? The Pharisees, who said that he cast out devils by Beelzebub, the prince of devils.

What did Herod the tetrarch think, when he heard of the fame of Jesus? He thought that Jesus was John the Baptist, risen from the dead.

Who were about to take Jesus by force and make him king? The 5000 men, whom he fed with five loaves and two small fishes, John 6:15.

Who did men say that Christ was? Some said he was John the Baptist; some, Elijah; others, Jeremiah, or one of the prophets, Mat. 16:14.

Lesson 36.

Who saw Christ transfigured? Peter, James, and John, Mat. 17.

Who appeared to them on the mount of transfiguration? Moses and Elijah.

Of what did they speak? Of Christ's death.

What did Jesus say, when little children were brought to him? Permit the little children to come unto me, and forbid them not; for of such is the kingdom of God.

How did he treat the little children, that were brought to him? He took them up in his arms, and blessed them, Mark 10:16.

Who went away sorrowful from Jesus? The rich young man, who vainly supposed he had kept all the commandments.

What was said by the officers, who were sent to take Christ? No man ever spoke like this man, John 7:46.

Lesson 37.

Where did Jesus weep? In sight of Jerusalem and at the grave of Lazarus.

How were the Pharisees affected, when the children cried Hosanna in the temple? They were greatly displeased, Mat. 21:15.

How did Christ spend his time on earth? In doing good, Acts 10:38.

Who were his greatest opposers? The Scribes and Pharisees.

Who denied that there is any resurrection? The Sadducees.

Whom did Jesus raise from the dead? The son of a widow of Nain, the daughter of Jairus, Lazarus, and probably others not particularly mentioned in the Bible.

What other miracles did he perform? He changed water into wine, stilled tempests, walked upon the sea, healed the sick, gave sight to the blind, hearing to the deaf, speech to the dumb, cast out devils, & etc. & etc.

Lesson 38.

When did Christ institute his holy supper? The night in which he was betrayed, 1 Cor. 11:23.

What act of great condescension did he perform at that time? He washed his disciples' feet.

Who leaned on Jesus' bosom at supper? John.

Where was Christ in agony? In the garden of Gethsemane.

What was the effect of his agony? His sweat became like great drops of blood falling down to the ground, Luke 22:44.

Who strengthened him at that time? And angel from heaven.

Who betrayed Christ? Judas.

How? With a kiss.

What was the reward of his iniquity? 30 pieces of silver.

Who cut off the ear of Malchus? Peter, John 18:10.

Who healed Malchus? Christ, Luke 22:51.

What was the conduct of the disciples, when Jesus was taken? The forsook him, and fled.

Lesson 39.

To whom was Jesus first led, after he was taken? To Annas.

To whom did Annas send him? To Caiaphas, the high priest.

Which of Christ's disciples denied him? Peter, Mat. 26:70.

What did Peter do when Christ then looked upon him? He went out, and wept bitterly.

Who was governor of Judea at that time? Pilate.

To whom did Pilate send Jesus? To Herod, the governor of Galilee, then at Jerusalem.

What did Herod do with him? He mocked him, and sent him back to Pilate.

Who sought to release Jesus? Pilate.

What did Pilate say of Christ's innocence? He said, I find no fault in him, John 19:4.

Why then did Pilate give sentence against him? To content the people, Mark 15:15.

What cruelties were inflicted upon Christ? He was scourged, mocked, struck, spit upon, reviled, blasphemed, and crucified.

Lesson 40.

Where was Christ crucified? Upon mount Calvary, near to Jerusalem on the west.

What did they give him to drink? Vinegar mingled with gall, Mat. 27:34.

Who were crucified with him? Two thieves or robbers, Mark 15:27.

For whom did Jesus pray, when he hung upon the cross? For his murderers, Luke 23:34.

What did he say to the penitent thief? Today you will be with me in Paradise.

How long was there miraculous darkness at that time? About three hours, Luke 23:44.

At what time in the day did Christ die? At the ninth hour, or, 3 o'clock in the afternoon.

What miraculous events took place, when Christ died? The veil of the temple was torn; the earth quaked; rocks split; and graves were opened, Mat. 27:51-52.

Lesson 41.

Who went to Pilate, and begged the body of Jesus? Joseph of Arimathea, Luke 23:52.

Who buried the body? Joseph and Nicodemus.

Where? In Joseph's new tomb, in a garden, Mat. 27:60.

What became of Judas? He hanged himself, fell headlong, burst asunder, and went to his own place, Mat. 27:5. Acts 1:15-18.

When did Christ rise from the dead? The third day after his death.

Who rolled away the stone, that had been placed at

the door of the tomb? An angel, Mat. 28:2.

What other miraculous events took place about that time? There was a great earthquake; and many bodies of dead saints arose, Mat. 27:52-53 & 28:2.

To whom did Christ first appear after the resurrection? To Mary Magdalene, Mark 16:9.

By how many brethren was he seen at once after his resurrection? Over 500, 1 Cor. 15:6.

How long did he continue upon earth after his resurrection? 40 days, Acts 1:3.

From what place did he ascend to heaven? Mount Olivet.

What is he doing in heaven? He is making intercession for his people, Heb. 7:25.

When and why will Christ come again? At the last day, to judge the world.

Lesson 42.

Who was chosen for an apostle in place of Judas? Matthias, Acts. 1:26.

How many were converted by means of Peter's preaching on the day of Pentecost? About 3000, Acts. 2:41.

Who were struck dead for lying to the Holy Spirit? Ananias and Saphira, Acts 5.

Who is the Holy Ghost, that is, the Holy Spirit? God, Acts 5:3-4.

Who was the first Christian martyr? Stephen, Acts 7.

Who guarded the clothes of those who were killing him? Saul of Tarsus, Acts. 22:20.

Why was Simon the sorcerer sharply rebuked by Peter? For offering to purchase the gift of the Holy

Spirit with money.

Who baptized the Eunuch of Ethiopia? Philip, Acts 8:26-39.

Who breathed out threatening and slaughter against the disciples of the Lord about that time? Saul of *Tarsus, Acts 9.*

Why did he journey to Damascus? To persecute saints.

What miraculous appearance did he see in the way? A light from heaven brighter than the sun.

How was he affected? He was struck blind to the earth, Acts 9:4.

What did Christ then say to him? Saul, Saul, why are you persecuting me?

How long was Saul at Damascus without eating, drinking, or seeing? Three days.

How did he spend the time? It is probable he spent it principally in praying, Acts. 9:11.

Whom did Christ send to restore Saul's sight? Ananias.

What was Saul afterwards called? Paul.

Lesson 43.

Where were the disciples of Christ first called Christians? At Antioch.

Who was the great apostle to the Gentiles? Paul, Rom. 11:13.

Who were called sons of thunder? James and John, Mark 3:17.

Who was a son of consolation? Barnabas.

Who raised Dorcas (also known as Tabitha) to life? Peter, Acts 9:36-40.

What devout centurion lived at Cesarea? Cornelius,

Acts. 10.

Who was sent to preach the gospel to him? Peter.

Who killed James, the brother of John? Herod.

What did Herod do to Peter at that time? Put him into prison. Acts 12.

How was Peter delivered? By an angel.

What miracle did Paul perform at Lystra? He healed a cripple, Acts 14:8-10.

Who was baptized with her household near Philippi? Lydia, Acts 16.

Why were Paul and Silas imprisoned at Philippi? For casting out a spirit of divination.

What did they do in prison? They prayed, and sang praises to God at midnight, Acts 16:25.

What miraculous events then took place? There was a great earthquake, the prison doors were opened, and the chains of all the prisoners were loosed, Acts 16.

What did the jailor do, when he saw the prison doors open? He drew his sword, to kill himself.

What did Paul say to him? Do yourself no harm, for we are all here.

What then took place? The jailor believed; and he and his household were baptized.

Lesson 44.

Who were converted by Paul's preaching at Athens? Dionysius and some others, Acts 17.

Who was an eloquent man, knowing only the baptism of John? Apollos.

Who explained to him the way of God more perfectly? Aquila and Priscilla, Acts 18:26.

Who made silver shrines for the goddess Diana at Ephesus? Demetrius.

How many Jews took an oath, not to eat nor drink until they had killed Paul? More than forty.

Who informed the chief captain of the conspiracy? Paul's nephew, Acts 23:16-22.

Who accused Paul before Felix? Tertullus, Acts 24.

Why did Felix tremble in the presence of Paul? He was affected by Paul's reasoning upon righteousness, temperance, and judgment to come.

Who succeeded Felix, as governor? Festus.

To whom did Paul appeal? To Cesar, Acts 25:11.

After Paul had related his conversion, what did Festus say to him? You are beside yourself! Much learning has made you mad! Acts 26:24.

What did Agrippa say to Paul at that time? You have almost persuaded me to be a Christian.

For what reason was Paul taken to Rome? To be judged by Cesar, to whom he had appealed.

What happened to him on his voyage to Rome? He was shipwrecked, Acts 27.

Upon what island was he cast? Upon Melita, supposed to be the same as Malta.

What happened to him there? A viper fastened upon his hand.

What did Paul do with the viper? He shook it off into the fire, Acts 28:5.

How long did Paul continue at Rome? At least two years.

How did he spend his time there? In preaching in the house, where he lived, Acts 28:30-31.

Lesson 45.

Who ran away from Philemon? Onesimus.

Why did he go back? He was converted, and sent

back by Paul.

Who made shipwreck concerning faith? Hymeneus and Alexander.

Why was John banished to the isle of Patmos? For the word of God and the testimony of Jesus Christ, Rev. 1:9.

Who appeared to John in Patmos? Christ.

For what purpose? To reveal to him things, that were to take place.

To whom was John directed to write? To the seven churches in Asia.

Who are concerned to know what the Spirit said to those churches? Those who have ears to hear.

Lesson 46.

Who is the Brightness of the Father's glory? Christ, Heb. 1:3.

Who is the Lord of lords and King of kings? Christ, Rev. *17:14.*

Who thought it not robbery to be equal with God? Christ, Phil. 2:6.

Who searches the searches minds and hearts? Christ, Rev. 2:23.

Who is the Root and the Offspring of David? Christ, Rev. 22:16.

Who is the First and the Last? Christ, Rev. 2:8.

Who is full of grace and truth? Christ, John 1:14.

Who is the Prince of peace? Christ, Is. 9:6.

Who is the Lamb of God? Christ, John 1:29, 36.

Who is the Prince of life? Christ, Acts 3:15.

Who is the Captain of salvation? Christ, Heb. 2:10.

Who is the Lion of the tribe of Judah? Christ, Rev. 5:5.

Who is the door of the sheep? Christ, John 10:7.

Who is the bread of life? Christ, John 6:48.

Who is the Author and Finisher of faith? Christ, Heb. 12:2.

Who is the Way, and the Truth, and the Life? Christ, John 14:6.

Who has the keys of hell and of death? Christ, Rev. 1:18.

Who is the great Shepherd of the sheep? Christ, Heb. 13:20.

Who is the true Vine? Christ, John 15:1.

Who is the believer's Life? Christ, Co. 3:4.

Who is the Head of the church? Christ, Col. 1:18.

Who is the Bridegroom of the church? Christ, Mat. 25:5.

Who is the Same yesterday, today, and forever? Christ, Heb. 13:8.

Who is altogether lovely? Christ, Song of Solomon 5:16.

THE WESTMINSTER ASSEMBLY'S SHORTER CATECHISM
WITH SHORT EXPLANATORY NOTES AND COPIOUS SCRIPTURE PROOFS AND ILLUSTRATIONS

1. What is the chief end of man?

Man's chief end is to glorify God,* and enjoy him forever.+

Chief End, That which ought to be man's chief aim and design, and which he should seek, as his chief happiness.

To glorify God, To do him honor, as the most glorious and most excellent Being, Ps. 50:23.

To enjoy God, To rejoice in his presence and in his love.

*I Cor. 10:31. Whether therefore ye eat, or drink, or whatsoever you do, do all to the glory of God.

Col. 3:23. And whatsoever ye do, do it heartily as to the Lord, and not unto men. Ps. 20:2 & 115:1. Is. 42:8. Dan.5:23, Mal.2:2. Matt. 5:16. Luke 2:14. John 12:28 & 13:31-32 & 17:4 & 15:8 & 21:19. Acts 12:23. Rom. 1:21 & 3:23. Gal. 1:24. 1 Pet. 4:11. Rev. 4:11.

+Ps 32:11 Be glad in the Lord and rejoice ye righteous; and shout for joy, all ye that are upright in heart.

Phil. 4:4. Rejoice in the Lord always; and again, I say, rejoice. Ps. 4:6 & 42:1-2 & 64:10 & 68:3 & 73:25-26. Phil. 3:1. Rev. 7:16-17.

2. What rule has God given, to direct us, how we may glorify and enjoy him?

The word of God, which is contained in the scriptures of the old and new testament,* is the only rule, to direct us, how we may glorify and enjoy him.+

The Scriptures of the old and new testament, The Bible.

*2 Tim. 3:16. All scripture is given by inspiration of God, and is profitable for doctrine, for reproof, for correction, for instruction in righteousness, Heb. 1:1-2. 2 Pet.1:21.

+John 5:39. Search the Scriptures; for in them ye think ye have eternal life; and they are they, which testify of me. John 14:6. Jesus saith unto him, I am the way, and the truth, and the life; no man cometh unto the Father but by me. Acts 4:12. I Cor. 3:11. Heb. 2:3.

3. What do the scriptures principally teach?

The scriptures principally teach, what man is to believe concerning God, and what duty God requires of man.

4. What is God?

God is a spirit,* infinite, eternal, and unchangeable, in his being, wisdom power, holiness, justice, goodness, and truth.+

A spirit, A being that has understanding and will; but no shape nor parts: nor can it be seen with the eyes.

Infinite, Without bound.

Eternal, Without beginning or end.

*John 4:24. God is a spirit; and they that worship him must worship him in spirit and in truth.

+Job 11:7. Canst thou by searching find out the Almighty unto perfection?

Ps. 90:2. Mal. 3:6. Ps. 139:1-12. James 1:17. 1 Kings 8:27. Heb. 4:13. Rom. 11:33. Acts 15:18. Col. 2:3. Deut. 32:4. Ps. 147:5. Ex. 34:6.

5. Are there more gods than one?

There is but one only, the living and true God.

Is. 45:22. Look unto me, and be ye saved, all the ends of the earth; for I am God, and there is none else.

6. How many persons are there in the Godhead?

There are three persons in the Godhead,* the Father,+ the Son,** and the Holy Ghost;++ and these three are one God, the same in substance, equal in power and glory.

Three persons in the Godhead, Three, to whom in personal terms, *I, thou, he* are applied.

*I John 5:7. For there are three, that bear record in heaven, the Father, the Word, and the Holy Ghost; and these three are one. Mat. 28:19. 2 Cor. 13:14. Gen. 1:26 & 3:27 & 11:7. Is.6:3. Rev. 4:8.

+Mat. 10:32. Whosoever therefore shall confess me before men, him will I confess also before my Father, which is in heaven. Mat. 11:27 & 15:13 & 18:10 & 25:34. **John 1:1, 14. In the beginning was the Word, and the Word was with God, and the Word was God. And the Word was made flesh, and dwelt among us, and we beheld his glory, the glory as of the only begotten of the Father, full of grace and truth. Mat. 8:29 & 14:33 & 27:43, 54. John 1:34 & 3:18 & 5:17-23 & 10:15-18, 29. 30, 36-38. Is. 7:14. Mat. 1:23. Is. 9:6. Hebrews 1:3, 8. 1 John 5:20. I Tim. 3:16. John 20:28. Phil. 2:5, 6, 10, 11. Heb. 13:8. Rev. 1:8 & 2:8. Eph. 4:10. Mat. 18:20 & 28:20. John 3:13. Rev. 2:23. John 2:24, 25 & 21:17. Heb. 1:6. Mat. 8:2 & 9:18 & 14:33 & 15:25 & 28:9. John 9:38. Luke 24:52. Acts 7:59.

++Acts 5:3-4. But Peter said, Ananias, why hath Satan filled thine heart to lie to the Holy Ghost—thou has not lied unto men but unto God. Gen. 1:2. Job 26:13 & 33:4. Ps. 104:30. Is. 40 13-14. Mat. 3:16. Luke 1:35. John 3:5 & 14:16, 17, 26 & 15:26 & 16:7-11, 13. Acts 2:4 & 15:28 & 16:6,7 & 20: 23 & 28:25. Is. 6:9. Rom 8:15-16, 26-27 & 9:1 & 15:16. I Cor. 2:10-11 & 6:19 & 12:1-13. Gal. 5:22-23. Eph. 2:18. 2 Thes. 2:13. Heb. 3:7-9. Ex. 17:7. Heb. 9:14 & 10:15-16.

7. What are the decrees of God?

The decrees of God are his eternal purpose, according to the counsel of his own will, whereby for his own glory he hath foreordained, whatsoever comes to pass.

Eph. 1:11 Being predestinated according to the purpose of him, who worketh all things after the counsel of his own will. 2 Sam. 17:14. Job 7:1 & 14:5, 14. Ps. 33:11. Prov. 19:21. Is. 14:24, 27 & 19:12 & 23:9 & 46:10-11 & 55:11. Jer. 32:19. Dan. 4:24, 35 & 8:19 & 9:24. Hab. 1:12. Zeph. 3:8. Mat. 24:22, 24, 31 & 26:24. Mark 13:20. Luke 18:7 & 22:22. John 6:39 & 10:16. Acts. 1:24 & 2:23 & 4:27 -28 & 17:26, 31. Rom. 8:28-33 & 9:11 & 11:5, 7. Eph. 1:4-5. Col. 3:12. I Thes. 1:4. 2 Thes. 2:13. I Tim. 5:21. 2 Tim. 2:10. Tit. 1:1. Heb. 6:17. 1 Pet. 1:2. Jude verse 4. Rev. 17:17.

8. How does God execute his decrees?

God executeth his decrees in the works of creation and providence.

Execute, Fulfill or bring to pass.

9. What is the work of creation?

The work of creation is God's making all things* of nothing+ by the word of his power in the space of six days, and all very good.**

The word of his power, His powerful word.

*Rev. 4:11. Thou has created all things; and for thy pleasure they are, and were created. Gen. 1. Prov. 16:4. Heb. 3:4.

+Heb. 11:3. Through faith we understand that the worlds were framed by the word of God; so that things, which are seen, were not made of things which do appear.

**Gen. 1:31. And God saw everything that he had made, and behold it was very good.

10. How did God create man?

God created man male and female after his own image, in knowledge, righteousness, and holiness, with dominion over his creatures.

Male and female, Man and woman.

Image of God, Likeness of God. Gen. 1:27. So God created man in his own image, in the image of God created he him, male and female created he them. Gen. 1:26-27, 31. Eccl. 7:29. Eph. 4:24. Col. 3:10.

11. What are God's works of providence?

God's works of providence are his most holy, wise, and powerful, preserving* and governing+ all his creatures and all their actions.

All their actions, Everything they do.

*Heb. 1:3. Upholding all things by the word of his power. Neh. 9:6. Job 7:20 & 10:12. Ps. 36:6. Dan. 5:23. Acts 17:28. Col. 1:17.

+Eph. 1:11. Being predestinated according to the purpose of him, who worketh all things after the counsel of his own will. Gen. 45:5,7. 2 Chron. 20:6. Ps. 47:2 & 103:19 & 145:13 & 147 & 148:8. Prov. 16:9, 33. Is. 10:5-7, 12, 15 & 14:24, 27. Dan. 4:3, 34. Joel 2:19, 20, 23, 25. Amos 4:6-13. Matt. 5:45 & 6:26, 30, 33 & 10:20. Phil. 2:13. James 1:17. 1 Pet. 3:22.

12. What special act of providence did God exercise toward man in the state, wherein he was created?

When God created man, he entered into a covenant of life with him, upon condition of perfect obedience, forbidding him to eat of the tree of knowledge of good and evil, upon pain of death.

13. Did our first parents continue in the state, wherein they were created?

Our first parents, being left to the freedom of their own will, fell from the state, wherein they were created, by sinning against God.

14. What is sin?

Sin is any want of conformity unto, or transgression of the law of God.*

Conformity to the law, Being and doing, what the law requires.

Transgression of the law, Being or doing, what the law forbids.

*I John 3:4. Whosoever committeth sin, transgresseth also the law; for sin is the transgression of the law. Rom. 3:20 & 7:7-11.

15. What was the sin, whereby our first parents fell

from the state, wherein they were created?

The sin, whereby our first parents fell from the state, wherein they were created, was their eating of the forbidden fruit.

Gen. 3:6. And when the woman saw that the tree was good for food, and that it was pleasant to the eyes, and a tree to be desired to make one wise, she took of the fruit thereof, and did eat; and gave also unto her husband with her, and he did eat. Gen. 2:16-17.

16. Did all mankind fall in Adam's first transgression?

The covenant being made with Adam, not only for himself , but for his posterity, all mankind, descending from him by ordinary generation, sinned in him, and fell with him in his first transgression.

Rom. 5:19. By one man's disobedience many were made sinners.

17. Into what state did the fall bring mankind?

The fall brought mankind into a state of sin and misery.

Rom. 5:12. By one man sin entered into the world, and death by sin; and so death passed upon all men, for that all have sinned.

18. Wherein consists the sinfulness of that state, whereinto man fell?

The sinfulness of that state, whereinto man fell, consists in the guilt of Adam's first sin, the want of original righteousness, and the corruption of his whole nature,* which is commonly called original sin, together with all actual transgressions, which proceed from it.

*Rom. 5:19 By one man's disobedience many were made sinners. I Cor. 15:22. In Adam all die. Gen. 6:5, 11-13 & 8:21. Job 14:4 & 15:16 & 25:5-6. Ps. 14:1-3 & 73:8-9 & 51:5 & 53:3 & 58:3. Prov. 1:22 & 27:22. Is. 1:5-6 & 53:6 & 59:7-8. Jer. 2:13 & 3:5 & 16:12 & 17:9 & 18:12. Mat. 3:7 & 8:22 & 12:34. Mark 7:21-22. John 3: 6, 19. Rom. 8:5-8. Gal. 5:19-21. Rom 1: 29-32 & 3:9-19 & 7:18. 2 Cor. 5:14. Eph.

2:1-3. Col. 2:13. Tit. 1:16 & 3:3. 1 Pet. 4:3. Ps. 110:1-2.

19. *What is the misery of that state whereinto man fell?*

All mankind by the fall lost communion with God,* are under his wrath+ and curse,** and so made liable to all the miseries of this life, to death itself, and to the pains of hell forever.++

*Gen. 3:8. And Adam and his wife hid themselves from the presence of the Lord among the trees of the garden.

+Eph. 2:3. And were by nature the children of wrath, even as others.

**Gal. 3:10. Cursed is everyone that continueth not in all things, which are written in the book of the law to do them.

++John 3:3. Except a man be born again he cannot see the kingdom of God he cannot see the kingdom of God. Mat. 25:46. And these shall go away into everlasting punishment. Job 31:3. Ps. 11:6 & 37:20 & 145:20. Prov. 10:24, 29 &11:21. Is. 3:11 & 50:11 & 66:24. Mat. 3:7, 10, 12. Luke 3:7, 9, 17. John 17:12. Luke 13: 23-28. Mat. 13:24-30, 40-42, 47-50 & 22:10-14 & 25:11-12, 30-46. John 8:2-24. Mat. 12:31-32. Mark 3:29. Luke 12:10, Mat. 10:28, 33 & 16:25-26 & 23:33. Mark 8:38 & 9:43-48 & 16:16. Luke 13:3 & 19:27. Acts 1:25. 1 Pet. 4:18. 2 Pet. 2:1, 3-4, 9, 12,17 & 3:7. Rom. 2:5-9:12. 2 Cor. 2: 15-16 & 5:10-11. Phil. 3:18-19. 2 Thes. 1:6-10. Heb. 2:3 & 10:26-31 & 12:25. James 1:15. I John 5:16-17. Rev. 1:7 & 14:10-11 & 20:10, 14 & 21:8 & 22:11-12, 19.

20. *Did God leave all mankind to perish in this state of sin and misery?*

God, having out of his mere good pleasure from all eternity elected some to everlasting life,* did enter into a covenant of grace, to deliver them out of this state of sin and misery, and to bring them into a state of salvation by a Redeemer.

Elected, Chosen.

Salvation, Deliverance of men from hell and bringing them to heaven.

*Eph. 1:4. According as he hath chosen us in him before the

foundation of the world, that we should be holy, and without blame before him in love. Acts 13:48. Rom. 8:28-30, 33 & 9:11 & 11:5, 7, 28. Eph. 1:4-5, 11. Matt. 20:23 & 24:22, 24, 31 & 25:34. Mark 10:40 7 13:20, 22, 27. Luke 18:7. Col. 3:12. 1 Thes. 1:4. 2 Thes. 2:13. 2 Tim. 1:9. Tit. 1:1. 1 Pet. 1:2. 2 Pet. 1:10. Rev. 13:8.

21. *Who is the Redeemer of God's elect?*

The only Redeemer of God's elect is the Lord Jesus Christ, who, being the eternal Son of God, became man,* and so was and continues to be God and man in two distinct natures and one person forever.

God's elect, Those whom God has chosen for his own people.
Jesus, A Savior. Mat. 1:21.
Christ, Anointed of God.
*John 1:1, 14. In the beginning was the Word, and the Word was with God, and the Word was God. And the Word was made flesh, and dwelt among us. [See scriptures referred to under question 6.]

22. *How did Christ being the Son of God, become man?*

Christ, the Son of God, became man, by taking to himself a true body and a reasonable soul, being conceived by the power of the Holy Ghost in the womb of the virgin Mary, and born of her, and yet without sin.

Heb. 2:14. Matt. 26:38. Luke 1: 31, 35. Heb. 7:26.

23. *What offices does Christ execute, as our Redeemer?*

Christ, as our Redeemer, executeth the office of a Prophet,* of a Priest,+ and of a King,** both in his state of humiliation and exaltation.

The offices of Christ, The special works or business, which the Father appointed him to perform.
*Deut. 18:15. Mat. 21:11. Luke 4:24 & 7:16 & 3:33 & 24:19. John 4:39 & 6:14 & 7:40 & 9:17. Acts 3:22-23 & 7:37. Heb. 1:2.
+Ps. 10:4. Heb. 2:17 & 3:1 & 4:14-15 & 5:5, 10 & 6:20 & 7:3, 20-28 & 8:1 & 9:11 & 10:21.

**Ps. 2:6 & 45:1, 6, 11, 14 & 89:36-37,. Is. 9:6-7 & 32:1. Jer. 23:5-6. Ezek. 37:24-25. Dan. 7:13-14. Mat. 21:5 & 22:11,13. Luke 1:32-33 & 19:38 & 22:29-30. John 1:49 & 1:13, 15 & 18:36. Zec. 9:9. 1 Tim.6:15. Rev. 17:14 & 19:16.

24: How does Christ execute the office of a Prophet

Christ executeth the office of a Prophet in revealing to us by his word and Spirit the will of God for our salvation.*

To reveal, To make known what was hidden.

The will of God, What God proposes and requires.

*John 1:18. No man hath seen God at any time; the only begotten Son, which is in the bosom of the Father, he had declared him.

25. How does Christ execute the office of a Priest?

Christ executeth the office of a Priest in his once offering up of himself, a sacrifice, to satisfy divine justice, and reconcile us to God,* and in making continual intercession for us.+

Sacrifice, Some living creature slain and offered up.

To satisfy divine justice, To answer for the dishonor, which the sin of man has done to the authority and justice of God, as Governor.

To reconcile, To make friends, to bring man into the favor of God.

Intercession, Pleading or praying for another.

*Heb. 9:26. But now once in the end of the world, he hath appeared, to put away sin by the sacrifice of himself. Is. 53:4-7. Dan. 9:26. Mat. 20:28 & 26:28. John 10:11, 15, 17. Acts 20:28. Rom. 5:6, 8-10, 12 & 6:10. I Cor. 15:3. 2 Cor. 5:14-15. Gal. 1:3-4 & 2:20. Eph. 1:7 & 2:13 & 5:2, 25. 1 Tim. 2:6. Tit. 2:14. Heb. 1:3 & 2:9 & 9:12, 14, 22 & 10:12, 14, 19-20 & 13:10, 12. 1 Pet. 2:21 & 3:18. 1 John 1:7, 9. Rev. 1:5 & 5:9 & 7:14.

+Heb. 7:25. He is able also to save them to the uttermost, that come unto God by him, seeing he ever liveth to make intercession for them. Is. 53:12. Rom 8:34. Heb. 9:24. 1 John 2:1.

26. How does Christ execute the office of a King?

Christ executeth the office of a King in subduing us to himself,* in ruling and defending us, and in restraining and conquering all his and our enemies.+

Subduing us to himself, Bringing our souls to obey Christ.

*Ps. 110:3. Thy people shall be willing in the day of thy power. Eph. 2:15, 12. Col. 1:21. Tit. 3:3.

+1 Cor. 15:25. For he must reign, til he hath put all enemies under his feet. Ps. 2:9. Rev. 3:21.

27. Wherein did Christ's humiliation consist?

Christ's humiliation consisted in his being born, and that in a low condition, in being made under the law,* in undergoing the miseries of this life,+ the wrath of God,** and the cursed death of the cross,++ in being buried and continuing under the power of death for a time.

Cursed death of the cross, So called, because it is written, cursed is every one that hangeth on a tree, Gal. *3:13, that is devoted to shame as well as to death.*

*Gal. 4:4. But when the fullness of time was come, God sent forth his Son, made of a woman, made under the law.

+Is. 53:3. He is despised and rejected of men, a man of sorrows and acquainted with grief.

**Mat. 27:46. And about the ninth hour Jesus cried with a loud voice, saying—My God, my God, why hast thou forsaken me?

++Phil. 2:8. He humbled himself, and became obedient unto death, even the death of the cross.

28. Wherein consists Christ's exaltation?

Christ's exaltation consisteth in his rising again from the dead on the third day, in ascending up into heaven, and sitting at the right hand of God the Father,* and in coming to judge the world at the last day.+

Sitting at the right hand of God, Having power and authority over all things given him by the Father.

*Mark 16:19. So then, after the Lord had spoken unto them, he was received up into heaven, and sat on the right hand of God.

+John 5:22. The Father judgeth no man; but hath committed all judgment unto the Son. Mat. 16:27 & 24:30 & 25:31-46. Mark 8:38 & 13:26 & 14: 62. Luke 9:26 & 21:27. Acts 1:11. 1 Thes. 1:10 & 3:13 & 4:16. 2 Thes. 1:7-10. Jude verse 14. Rev. 1:7 & 22:12, 20. Ps. 50:3.

29. How are we made partakers of the redemption, purchased by Christ?

We are made partakers of the redemption, purchased by Christ, by the effectual application of it to us by the Holy Spirit.*

Redemption, Deliverance from sin and misery.

Effectual application of the redemption of Christ, The powerful conveying of the benefits of this redemption to us.

*Tit. 3:5-6. Not by words of righteousness, which we have done, but according to his mercy he saved us, by the washing of regeneration, and renewing of the Holy Ghost; which he shed on us abundantly through Jesus Christ our Savior.

30. How does the Spirit apply to us the redemption, purchased by Christ?

The Spirit applieth to us, the redemption, purchased by Christ, by working faith in us,* and thereby uniting us to Christ+ in our effectual calling.**

Uniting us to Christ, Making us one with Christ, as the head and members are one.

*Eph. 2:8. By grace are ye saved through faith; and that not of yourselves; it is the gift of God.

+Eph. 3:17. That Christ may dwell in your hearts by faith.

**1 Cor. 1:9. God is faithful, by whom ye were called unto the fellowship of his Son Jesus Christ our Lord.

31. What is effectual calling?

Effectual calling is a work of God's Spirit,* whereby convincing us of our sin and misery, enlightening our minds in the knowledge of Christ, and renewing our wills,+ he doth persuade and enable us to embrace Jesus Christ, freely offered to us in the gospel.

Renewing our wills, Changing our old sinful inclinations, and giving us, new and holy inclinations.

*2 Tim. 1:9. Who hath saved us, and called us with an holy calling.

+Ps. 110:3. Thy people shall be willing in the day of thy power.

Ezek. 36:26. A new heart also will I give you, and a new spirit will I put within you, and I will take the stony heart out of your flesh, and I will give you an heart of flesh.

32. What benefits do they, that are effectually called, partake of in this life?

They, that are effectually called, do in this life partake of justification,* adoption,+ and sanctification,** and the several benefits, which in this life do either accompany, or flow from them.

To justify, To pardon sin, and to receive a person into favor of God, as though he were righteous.

To adopt, To take one that is a stranger to be a son or daughter.

To sanctify, To make our sinful nature holy.

*Rom. 8:30. Moreover, whom he did predestinate, then he also called; and whom he called, them he also justified; and whom he justified, them he also glorified.

+Eph. 1:5. Having predestinated us unto the adoption of children by Jesus Christ to himself.

**1 Cor. 1:30. Of him are ye in Christ Jesus, who of God is made unto us wisdom, and righteousness, and sanctification, and redemption.

33. What is justification?

Justification is an act of God's free grace,* wherein he pardoneth all our sins,+ and accepteth us, as righteous in his sight,** only for the righteousness of Christ,++ imputed to us, and received by faith alone.***

Free grace, Free favor to the guilty.

Imputed to us, Reckoned to our account.

*Rom. 3:24. Being justified freely by his grace, through the redemption that is in Christ Jesus.

+Eph. 1:7. In whom we have redemption through his blood, the forgiveness of sins, according to the riches of his grace.

**2 Cor. 5:21. For he hath made him to be sin for us, who knew no sin, that we might be made the righteousness of God in him.

++Rom. 5:19. As by one man's disobedience many were made sinners; so by the obedience of one shall many be made righteous.

***Rom. 3:28. Therefore we conclude, that a man is justified by faith without the deeds of the law.

34. What is adoption?

Adoption is an act of God's free grace, whereby we are received into the number, and have a right to all the privileges of the sons of God.

1 John 3:1. Behold what manner of love the Father hat bestowed upon us, that we should be called the sons of God. Gen. 6:2. Hosea 1:10. John 1:12. Rom 8:15-17. 2 Cor. 6:17-18. Gal. 3:26 & 4:4-7. Phil. 2:15.

35. What is sanctification?

Sanctification is a work of God's Spirit,* whereby we are renewed in the whole man after the image of God,+ and are enabled more and more to die unto sin, and live unto righteousness.**

The image of God, The likeness of his holiness.

To die unto sin, To forsake sin in heart and life.

To live unto righteousness, To follow after righteousness in heart and life.

*2 Thes. 2:13. God hath from the beginning chosen you to salvation through sanctification of the Spirit, and belief of the truth.

+Eph. 4:24. And that ye put on the new man, which after God is created in righteousness and true holiness. Gen. 1: 26-27.

**Rom. 8:1. There is therefore now no condemnation to them which are in Christ Jesus, who walk not after the flesh but after the Spirit.

36. What are the benefits, which in this life do either accompany, or flow from justification, adoption, and sanctification?

The benefits, which in this life do either accompany, or flow from justification, adoption, and sanctification, are assurance of God's love, peace of conscience, joy in the Holy Ghost, increase of grace,* and perseverance therein to the end.+

Joy in the Holy Ghost, Holy rejoicing, wrought in us by the Spirit of God.

Increase of grace, Growing in holiness.
Perseverance, Continuance.
*Prov. 4:18. The path of the just is as the shining light, that shineth more and more unto the perfect day.
+Rom. 8:29-30. For whom he did fore know, he also did predestinate, to be conformed to the image of his Son, that he might be the first born among many brethren. Moreover, whom he did predestinate, them he also called; and whom he called, them he also justified; and whom he justified, them he also glorified. John 4:14 & 6:37 & 10:27-29. 1 Pet. 1:5. Prov. 10:25. 1 Thes. 5:9, & 10:24. 2 Thes. 3:3. Phil. 1:6. 1 Cor. 1:8-9 & 10:13. Job 17:9. Ps. 125:2. Mt. 7:24-25. John 6:27, 35, 39-40, 54-58. Col. 3:3. Heb. 10:39. 1 Pet. 1:5.

37. What benefits do believers receive from Christ, at their death?

The souls of believers are at their death made perfect in holiness,* and do immediately pass into glory;+ and their bodies, being still united to Christ, do rest in their graves till the resurrection.

Glory, State of honor and happiness in heaven.
The resurrection, The rising from the dead at the last day.
*Heb. 12:23. To the spirits of just men made perfect.
+Phil. 1:23. I am in a strait betwixt two, having a desire to depart, and to be with Christ; which is far better. Rev. 14:13.

38. What benefits will believers receive from Christ at the resurrection?

At the resurrection believers, being raised up to glory, will be openly acknowledged and acquitted in the day of judgment,* and made perfectly blessed in the full enjoyment of God to all eternity.+

Acknowledged, Owned for the children of God.
Acquitted, Freed from all charges of sin.
*Mat. 10:32. Whoever therefore shall confess me before men, him will I confess also before my Father, which is in heaven.
+1 Thes. 4:17. And so shall we ever be with the Lord. Ps. 16:11. In thy presence is fullness of joy; at thy right hand there are pleasures for evermore. Ps. 73:24. Prov. 4:1, 8. Dan. 12:2-3. Mat. 5:12 & 13:43 &

19:29, Luke 18:29-30. John 3:14-16 & 4:14, 36 & 5:28-29 & 6:27, 54 & 10:28 & 12:25-26 & 17:2, 24. Rom. 6:23 & 8:30. 1 Cor. 2:9 & 13:12 & 15:41-42. 2 Cor. 5:1, 8. Phil. 1: 21, 23. 2 Tim. 4:8. 1 Pet. 1:3-4 & 5:4. Rev. 2:10, 17, 26-28 & 3:5, 12, 21 & 7:9-17 & 21:4.

39. *What is the duty, which God requires of man?*

The duty, which God requires of man, is obedience to his revealed will.

Mic. 6:8. What doth the Lord require of thee, but to do justly, and to love mercy, and to walk humbly with God.

40. *What did God at first reveal to man for the rule of his obedience?*

The rule, which God at first revealed to man for his obedience, was the moral law.

Moral law, The law, which directs our manners or our duty to God and man.

41. *Where is the moral law summarily comprehended?*

The moral law is summarily comprehended in the ten commandments.

Summarily comprehended, Contained in short.

42. *What is the sum of the ten commandments?*

The sum of the ten commandments is to love the Lord our God with all our heart, with all our soul, with all our strength, and with all our mind, and our neighbor, as ourselves.

Mat. 22:37-40.

43. *What is the preface of the ten commandments?*

The preface of the ten commandments is in these words, I am the Lord thy God, who have brought thee out of the land of Egypt, out of the house of bondage.

Egypt, the house of bondage, The land where the Israelites were made bondmen.

44. What does the preface of the ten commandments teach us?

The preface of the ten commandments teacheth us that, because God is the Lord and our God and Redeemer, therefore we are bound to keep all his commandments.

45. What is the first commandment?

The first commandment is, Thou shalt have no other gods before me.

Ex. 20:3 & 15:11. Deut. 5:7 & 6:14. Josh. 24:18-24. 2 Kings 17:35. Ps. 29:2 & 73:25 & 81:9. Is. 26:4 & 43:10 & 44:8. Jer. 25:6. Mal. 1:6. Mat. 4:10. 1 Cor. 8:4, 6. Eph. 5:5.

46. What is required in the first commandment?

The first commandment requireth us to know* and acknowledge God, to be the only true God, and our God, and to worship and glorify him accordingly.

*Job 22:21. Acquaint now thyself with him, and be at peace. Deut. 4:35. 1 Kings 8:43. 1 Chron. 28:9. Jer. 9:24 & 31:34. Hos. 4:1. Rom. 1:28. 1 Cor. 15:34.

47. What is forbidden in the first commandment?

The first commandment forbiddeth the denying, or not worshipping and glorifying the true God, as God, and our God, and, the giving of that worship and glory to any other, which are due to him alone.

48. What are we specially taught by these words (before me) in the first commandment?

These words *(before me)* in the first commandment teach us that God, who seeth all things, taketh notice of, and is much displeased with the sin of having any other god.

Ps. 44:20-21. If we have forgotten the name of our God, or stretched out our hands to a strange god, shall not God search this out?

49. What is the second commandment?

The second commandment is, Thou shalt not make unto thee any graven image, nor any likeness of anything, that is in heaven above, or that is in earth beneath, or that is in the waters under the earth; thou shalt not bow down thyself to them, nor serve them;* for I the Lord they God, am a jealous+ God, visiting the iniquity of fathers upon children unto the third and fourth generation of them that hate me; and showing mercy unto thousands of them that love me, and keep my commandments.

Graven image, An image fashioned with a tool.

Jealous, Highly concerned for his own honor.

Visiting the iniquity, Punishing the sin.

*Ex. 20:4 & 32:1, 8 23-24, 35 & 34:17. Deut. 4:15-19, 23-26 & 5:8 & 7:5 & 9:16 & 16:22 & 27:15. 1 Kings 14:5-16, 22-23. 2 Kings 17:15-18 & 21:7, 10-12, 2 Chron. 28:1-5. Ps. 78:58-64 & 97:7. Is. 40:18-25 & 42:8 & 44:9-20. Jer. 8:19 & 10:8, 14. Ezek. 7:20-22 & 8:12, 18. Dan. 3:13-18. Hos. 13:2-3. Acts. 17:29. Rom. 1:23-25 & 11:4.

+Ex 34:14. Deut. 4:24 & 16:15 & 32:21. Josh. 24:19. Ps. 78:58. Ezek. 8:3. Nah. 1:2. 1 Cor. 10:22.

50. What is required in the second commandment?

The second commandment requireth the receiving, observing, and keeping pure and entire all such religious worship and ordinances, as God hath appointed in his word.*

Pure, Without mixture of the inventions of men.

Entire, Without omitting any part of what God has appointed.

*Deut. 12:32. What thing soever I command you, observe to do it; thou shalt not add thereto, nor diminish from it. Mat. 28:20. Teaching them to observe all things whatsoever I commanded you.

51. What is forbidden in the second commandment?

The second commandment forbiddeth the worshipping of God by images, or in any other way, not appointed in his word.

52. What are the reasons, annexed to the second commandment?

The reasons annexed to the second commandment, are God's sovereignty over us, his property in us, and the zeal he hath for his own worship.

Annexed, Joined.
Sovereignty, Highest dominion and authority.
Zeal, Warm concern.

53. What is the third commandment?

The third commandment is, Thou shalt not take the name of the Lord thy God in vain;* for the Lord will not hold him guiltless, that taketh his name in vain.

Take God's name in vain, Use it in a trifling manner.
*Lev. 19:12 & 24:10-16. Deut. 5:11 & 23:21-23. Ps. 15:4. Prov. 30:8-9. Ec. 5:4-6. Jer. 4:2 & 5:2, 9 & 7:9-10 & 23:10. Hos. 4:2 & 10:4. Zec. 5:3-4 & 8:17. Mat. 5:33-37 & 26:74-75. James 5:12.

54. What is required in the third commandment?

The third commandment requireth a holy and reverend use of God's names, titles, attributes, ordinances, word, and works.

Reverend use, Using with holy fear.
Names of God, Such as Lord, Jehovah, the Almighty, etc.
Titles of God, Such as holy One, high and lofty One, Judge of all the earth.
Attributes, The perfections and properties of God; such as wisdom, power, holiness, etc.

55. What is forbidden in the third commandment?

The third commandment forbiddeth all profaning or

abusing of anything whereby God maketh himself known.

Profaning or abusing, Using it for any trifling or sinful purposes or casting any dishonor upon it.

56. *What is the reason, annexed to the third commandment?*

The reason annexed to the third commandment, is, that however the breakers of this commandment may escape punishment from men, yet the Lord our God will not suffer them to escape his righteous judgment.

57. *What is the fourth commandment?*

The fourth commandment is, Remember the Sabbath day, to keep it holy;* six days shalt thou labor, and do all thy work; but the seventh day is the Sabbath of the Lord thy God; in it thou shalt not do any work, thou, nor thy son, nor thy daughter, thy man servant, nor thy maid servant, nor thy cattle, nor thy stranger that is within thy gates; for in six days the Lord made all that in them is, and rested the seventh day; wherefore the Lord blessed the Sabbath day, and hallowed it.

Hallowed, Sanctified or set apart for holy use.

Gen. 2:3. Ex. 16:23-30 & 31:13-17. Lev. 19:3, 30 & 23:3 & 26:2. Deut. 5:12-15. Neh. 13:15-22. Is. 56:4-7 & 58:13-14. Ezek. 20:12.

58. *What is required in the fourth commandment?*

The fourth commandment requireth keeping holy to God such set times, as he hath appointed in his word, expressly one whole day in seven, to be a holy Sabbath to himself.

59. *Which day of the seven has God appointed to be the weekly Sabbath?*

From the beginning of the world to the resurrection of Christ, God appointed the seventh day of the week to be the weekly Sabbath;* and the first day of the week ever since, to continue to the end of the word, which is the Christian Sabbath.+

*Gen. 2:3. And God blessed the seventh day, and sanctified it; because that in it he had rested from all his work, which God created and made.

+Acts 20:7. Upon the first day of the week, when the disciples came together to break bread, Paul preached unto them. I Cor. 16:2. Rev. 1:10.

60. How is the Sabbath to be sanctified?

The Sabbath is to be sanctified by a holy resting of all that day, even from such worldly employments and recreations, as are lawful on other days,* and by spending the whole time in public and private exercises of God's worship,+ except so much, as is to be taken up in works of necessity and mercy.**

Sanctified, Spent in a holy manner.

*Lev. 23:3. Six days shall work be done; but the seventh day is the Sabbath of rest, an holy convocation; ye shall do no work therein.

+Acts 17:2. And Paul, as his manner was, went in unto them, and three Sabbath days reasoned with them out of the scriptures. Lev. 19:30. Mark 6:2. Luke 4:16, 31. Acts 13:14-16, 27, 42, 44 & 15:21 & 17:2-3 & 18:4.

**Mat. 12:1-13. Mark 2:27. Luke 13:15-16 & 14:3-5. John 5:10-11 & 7:22-23 & 9:14.

61. What is forbidden in the fourth commandment?

The fourth commandment forbiddeth the omission or careless performance of the duties required, and the profaning of the day by idleness, or by doing that, which is in itself sinful, or by unnecessary thoughts, words, or works, about worldly employments or recreations.

62. What are the reasons annexed to the fourth commandment?

The reasons, annexed to the fourth commandment, are God's allowing us six days of the week for our own employment, his challenging a special property in the seventh, his own example, and his blessing the Sabbath day.

Challenging, Claiming.

63. What is the fifth commandment?

The fifth commandment is, Honor thy father and thy mother, that thy days may be long in the land, which the Lord thy God giveth thee. Ex. 21:15, 17. Lev. 19:3 & 20:9. Deut. 5:16 & 21:18-21 & 27:16. 1 Kings 2:19. Prov. 1:8-9 & 6:20 & 15:6 & 19:26 & 20:20 & 23:22-25 & 30:17. Is. 3:5. Jer. 35.18-19. Mal. 1:6. Mat. 15:4-6 & 19:19. Mark 7:10-12. Luke 18:20. Eph. 6:1-3. 1 Tim. 5:1-2, 4.

64. What is required in the fifth commandment?

The fifth commandment requireth the preserving of the honor, and performing of the duties, belong to everyone in their several places and relations, as superiors, inferiors, and equals.

65. What is forbidden in the fifth commandment?

The fifth commandment forbiddeth the neglecting of, or doing anything against the honor and duty, belonging to everyone in their several places and relations.

66. What is the reason annexed to the fifth commandment?

The reason, annexed to the fifth commandment, is a promise of long life and prosperity (as far as it shall serve for God's glory and their own good) to all such as keep this commandment.

Eph. 6:2-3. Honor thy father and mother, which is the first commandment with promise, that it may be well with thee, and thou mayest live long on the earth.

67. What is the sixth commandment?
Sixth commandment is, Thou shalt not kill.
Gen. 4:8-15 & 9:6 & 27:45 & 49:6. Ex. 21:14, 20. Lev. 24:17, 21. Num. 35:16-21, 31-34. Deut. 5:17 & 19:11-13. 2 Sam. 12:9-10. 2 Kings 21:16. Ps. 10:8-10. Prov. 1:10-19. Is. 1:15. Jer. 26:15. Mat. 5:21-22. John 8:44. Rom 13:9. James 2:11 & 4:1-2. 1 John 3:12, 15. Rev. 17:6 & 22:15.

68. What is required in the sixth commandment?
The sixth commandment requireth all lawful endeavors to preserve our own lives and the lives of others.

69. What is forbidden in the sixth commandment?
The sixth commandment forbiddeth the taking away of our own lives, or the life of our neighbor unjustly, and whatsoever tendeth thereunto.

70. What is the seventh commandment?
The seventh commandment is, Thou shalt not commit adultery. Lev. 18:20 & 20:10. 2 Sam. 12:9-11. Ps. 50:18. Prov. 2:16-19 & 6:24-35 & 7:5-27. Jer. 5:8-9 & 13:27 & 23:14 & 29:22-23. Mat. 5:27-28 & 19:9. Mark 10:11-12. Rom. 7:2-3. Gal. 5:19. Heb. 13:4. 2 Pet. 2:14, 18. Rev. 2:20-22 &21:8 & 22:15.

71. What is required in the seventh commandment?
The seventh commandment requireth the preservation of our own and our neighbor's chastity in heart, speech, and behavior.

72. What is forbidden in the seventh commandment?

The seventh commandment forbiddeth all unchaste thoughts, words, and actions.

Mat. 5:28. Whosoever looketh on a woman to lust after her, hath committed adultery with her already in his heart.

73. What is the eighth commandment?

The eighth commandment is, Thou shalt not steal.
Ex. 21:16 & 22:1, 7, 9. Lev. 19:11, 13, 3-36. Deut. 5:19 & 23:24-25 & 24:7. Ps. 50:18. Jer. 7:8-11. Zec. 5:3. Mat. 15:19 & 19:18 & 21:13. John 12:6. Rom. 13:9. 1 Cor. 6:10. Eph. 4:28.

74. What is required in the eighth commandment?

The eighth commandment requireth the lawful procuring and furthering of the wealth and outward estate of ourselves and others.

75. What is forbidden in the eighth commandment?

The eighth commandment forbiddeth whatsoever doth or may unjustly hinder our own or our neighbor's wealth or outward estate.

76. What is the ninth commandment?

The ninth commandment is, Thou shalt not bear false witness against thy neighbor. Ex. 23:7. Deut. 5:20 & 19:16-19. 1 Kings 21:9-13. Ps. 115:1, 3 & 50:20 & 101:5. Prov. 10:18 & 19:5, 9. Mat. 26:59-61. Eph. 4:31. 1 Tim. 3:11. 2 Tim. 3:3. Tit. 2:3. James 4:11. 1 Pet. 2:1. Rev. 12:10.

77. What is required in the ninth commandment?

The ninth commandment requireth the maintaining and promoting of truth between man and man,* and of our own and our neighbor's good name, especially in witnessbearing.

*Zec. 8:16. Speak ye every man the truth to his neighbor.

78. What is forbidden in the ninth commandment?

The ninth commandment forbiddeth whatsoever is prejudicial to truth, or injurious to our own or our neighbor's good name.

79. What is the tenth commandment?
The tenth commandment is, Thou shalt not covet thy neighbor's house, thou shalt not covet thy neighbor's wife, nor his man servant, nor his maid servant, nor his ox, nor his ass, nor anything that is thy neighbor's.*
Covet, Sinfully or unreasonably desire.
*Gen. 3:6 & 14:23. Deut. 5:21. Josh. 7:21. 1 Kings 21:1-16. 2 Kings 5:20. Ps. 10:3. Ec. 5:10. Is. 56:11 & 57:17. Jer. 22:17. Mic. 2:2. Hab. 2:9. Luke 12:15 & 16:14. John 12:6. Acts 20:33. Rom. 7:7. 1 Cor. 5:10 & 6:10. Eph. 5:5. 1 Tim. 6:6-10. Heb. 13:5. James 1:14-15 & 4:1-2. 2 Pet. 2:14-15. 1 John 2:16.

80. What is required in the tenth commandment?
The tenth commandment requireth full contentment with our own condition,* with a right and charitable frame of spirit toward our neighbor, and all that is his.
Charitable, Loving or bearing good will to another.
*Heb. 13:5. Let your conversation be without covetousness; and be content with such things, as ye have. Luke 3:14. Phil. 4:11. 1 Tim. 6:6, 8.

81. What is forbidden in the tenth commandment?
The tenth commandment forbiddeth all discontentment with our own estate, envying or grieving at the good of our neighbor, and all inordinate motions and affections to anything that is his.
Discontentment, A temper of mind unquiet or uneasy in our own state.
Envying, Being uneasy at another's welfare.
Inordinate motions and affections, Unreasonable and ungoverned desires and wishes.

82. Is any man able perfectly to keep the

commandments of God?

No mere man since the fall is able in this life perfectly to keep the commandments of God, but daily doth break them in thought, word, and deed.

Ec. 7:20. There is not a just man upon earth, that doeth good and sinneth not. 1 Kings 8:46. 2 Chron. 6:36. Job 15:14-16. Ps. 130:3 & 143:2. Prov. 20:9. James 3:2.

83. Are all transgressions of the law equally heinous?

Some sins in themselves, and by reason of several aggravations, are more heinous in the sight of God, than others.*

Heinous, Hateful.

Aggravation, That which makes an offense more grievous and faulty.

*John 19:11. Therefore he that delivered me unto thee hath the greater sin. Luke 10:11-14 & 12:47-48. John 15:22, 24. James 4:17.

84. What does every sin deserve.

Every sin deserves God's wrath and curse both in this life and in that which is to come.

Gal. 3:10. Cursed is everyone that continueth not in all the things which are written in the book of the law to do them.

85. What does God require of us, that we may escape his wrath and curse, due to us for sin?

To escape the wrath and curse of God, due to us for sin, God requireth of us faith in Jesus Christ,* repentance unto life+ with a diligent use of all outward means, whereby Christ communicateth to us the benefits of redemption.

Communicate, Give or bestow.

Benefits of redemption, Blessings of the gospel, procured by Christ.

*John 3:16. God so loved the world, that he gave his only begotten Son, that whosoever believeth in him should not perish, but have everlasting life. Mark 16:16. John 1:12 & 6:40, 47 & 11:25-26 & 12:44-

46 & 20:31. Acts 16:31. Rom. 5:1-2. Gal. 3:6. Heb. 10:39. 1 John 5:1.
John 3:18-19, 36 & 8:24.

+Luke 13:3, 5. Except ye repent, ye shall all likewise perish.
1 Kings 8:47-50. Job 42:6. Ps. 7:11-12. Ezek. 14:6 & 18:21 & 36:31.
Mat. 3:2 & 4:17 & 9:13 & 11:20. Mark 1:15. & 2:17 & 6:12.
Luke 5:32 & 15:7 & 16:30 & 24:47. Acts 2:38 & 3:19 & 8:22 & 17:30
& 20:21 & 26:20. 2 Cor. 7:9-10. 2 Pet. 3:9. Rev. 2:5, 16, 21-22.

86. What is faith in Jesus Christ?

Faith in Jesus Christ, is a saving grace,* whereby we receive and rest upon him alone for salvation, as he is offered to us in the gospel.

*Heb. 10:39. We are not of them, who draw back unto perdition, but of them, that believe to the saving of the soul.

87. What is repentance unto life?

Repentance unto life is a saving grace, whereby a sinner out of a true sense of his sin and apprehension of the mercy of God in Christ doth with grief and hatred of his sin turn from it unto God with full purpose of, and endeavors after new obedience.

88. What are the outward and ordinary means, whereby Christ communicateth to us the benefits of redemption?

The outward and ordinary means, whereby Christ communicateth to us the benefits of redemption, are his ordinances, especially the word, sacraments, and prayer; all which are made effectual to the elect for salvation.*

The Word, The word of God contained in the scriptures.

*Acts 2:41-42. Then they that gladly received his word were baptized; and the same day there were added unto them about three thousand souls. And they continued steadfastly in the apostles' doctrine and fellowship, and in breaking of bread, and in prayers.

89. How is the word made effectual to salvation?

The spirit of God maketh the reading, but especially

the preaching of the word, an effectual mean of convincing and converting sinners, and of building them up in holiness and comfort through faith unto salvation.*

To convince sinners, To make them know their sin and danger.

To convert sinners, To turn their hearts to love God, and trust in Christ.

Build them up, Make them increase.

*Ps. 19:7 The law of the Lord is perfect, converting the soul; the testimony of the Lord is sure, making wise the simple. Luke 8:11, 15. John 8:31-32 & 15:3, 11 & 17:17, 19. Rom. 10:14, 17. James 1:21. 1 Pet. 1:22-23.

90. How is the word to be read and heard, that it may become effectual to salvation?

That the word may become effectual to salvation, we must attend thereunto with diligence, preparation, and prayer, receive it with faith* and love, lay it up in our hearts, and practice it in our lives.+

*Heb. 4:2. But the word preached did not profit them, not being mixed with faith in them that heard it.

+James 1:25. But whoso looketh into the perfect law of liberty, and continueth therin, he being not a forgetful hearer, but a doer of the work, this man shall be blessed in his deed. Job 34:11. Ps. 62:12. Prov. 24:12. Ec. 12:14. Is. 3:10. Jer. 17:10 & 32:19. Mat. 5:16 & 7:17 & 16:27. John 15:1-8. Acts 9:36 & 10:38. 2 Cor. 5:10 & 9:8. Eph. 2:10 & 6:8. Col. 1:10. 1 Tim. 2:10 & 5:10 & 6:18. 2 Tim. 2:21 & 3:16-17. Tit. 2:7, 14 & 3:1, 8, 14. Heb. 10:24 & 13:16, 21. James 2:17. 1 Pet. 1:17 & 2:12. Rev. 2:2, 9, 13, 19, 23 & 3:1, 8, 15 & 14:13 & 20:12 & 22:12.

91. How do the sacraments become effectual means of salvation?

The sacraments become effectual means of salvation, not from any virtue in them, or in him that doth administer them* but only by the blessing of Christ, and the working of the Spirit in them, who by faith receive them.

*1 Cor. Neither is he, that planteth, anything, neither he, that watereth; but God that giveth the increase.

92. *What is a sacrament?*

A sacrament is a holy ordinance, instituted by Christ, wherein by sensible signs Christ and the benefits of the new covenant are represented, sealed, and applied to believers.

Instituted, Appointed, or commanded.

Sensible signs, Marks or tokens, that are perceived by the senses of seeing, feeling, tasting.

New Covenant, The covenant of grace or the gospel.

Sealed, Confirmed or made sure to us, as the possession of a house or land is made sure by a seal set to a writing.

93. *What are the sacraments of the New Testament!*

The sacraments of the New Testament are baptism and the Lord's supper. Mark 16:16. 1 Cor. 11:23-26.

94. *What is Baptism?*

Baptism is a sacrament, wherein the washing with water in the name of the Father, and of the Son, and of the Holy Ghost, doth signify and seal our ingrafting into Christ, our partaking of the benefits of the covenant of grace, and our engagement to be the Lord's.

Ingrafting into Christ, Union to Christ.

To be the Lord's, To be entirely devoted to the service of Christ.

95. *To whom is baptism to be administered?*

Baptism is not to be administered to any who are out of the visible church, till they profess their faith in Christ and obedience to him; but the infants of such, as are members of the visible church, are to be baptized.

Visible church, All that profess and apparently practice the true religion are members of the visible church. It is called visible; because it is to be seen by men; whereas the invisible church is made up of those, who have true religion in the heart, which God only knows and sees.

96. *What is the Lord's supper?*

The Lord's supper is a sacrament, wherein by giving and receiving bread and wine according to Christ's appointment his death is showed forth;* and the worthy receivers are, not after a corporal and carnal manner, but by faith made partakers of his body and blood, with all his benefits, to their spiritual nourishment and growth in grace.

Partakers of his body and blood, Partakers of the benefits of his death.

*Luke 22:19-20. And he took bread, and gave thanks, and brake it, and gave unto them saying, This is my body which is given for you; this do in remembrance of me. Likewise also the cup after supper saying, This cup is the new testament in my blood, which is shed for you. John 6:32-35, 41, 48, 50-58.

97. What is required in the worthy receiving of the Lord's supper?

It is required of them, who would worthily partake of the Lord's supper, that they examine themselves of their knowledge to discern the Lord's body, of their faith to feed upon him, of their repentance, love and new obedience, lest, coming unworthily, they eat and drink judgment to themselves.

To discern the Lord's body, To understand the design of the ordinance.

To feed upon Christ by faith, To derive blessings from him by trusting in him.

Eat and drink judgment, Expose themselves to the judgment of God.

98. What is prayer?

Prayer is the offering up of our desires to God for things agreeable to his will, in the name of Christ, with confession of our sins, and thankful acknowledgment of his mercies.

99. What rule has God given for our direction in prayer?

The whole word of God is of use to direct us in prayer;* but the special rule of direction is that form of prayer, which Christ taught his disciples, commonly called The Lord's Prayer.

*A considerable part of the book of Psalms is peculiarly adapted to direct, assist, and encourage us in prayer; likewise the following passages. Gen. 17:13 & 18:23-32 & 19:29 & 20:17 & 24:12-14, 42-52 & 32:9-12, 24-28. Ex. 17:11-12 & 32: 11-14, 30-32 & 33:12-13. Num. 14:13-22. Deut. 3:23-25. Josh. 10:12-14. Judg. 13:8-9 & 15:18-19 & 16:28-30. 1 Sam. 1:10-11 & 8:6 & 12:19, 23. 2 Sam. 7:18-29. 1 Kings 8:22. 2 Kings 19:14-19. 2 Chron. 7:14-15 & 14:9-12 & 20:5-12 & 33:12-13. Ezra 8:21-23 & 9:5-15. Neh. 1:4-11 & 9:4-38. Prov. 15:8, 29 & 28:9. Is 1:15 & 29:13-14 & 30:19. Hos. 12:3-4. Joel 2:15-27. Jonah 2:1-10. Hab. 3:2. Mat. 6:5-8. & 7:7-11 & 11:25 & 14:23. Mark 11:25. Luke 1:10 & 2:37 & 6:12 & 18:1-14 & 21:36 & 22:31-32. John 9:31 & 14:13 & 15:7, 16 & 16:23 & 17:1-26. Mat. 26:39-44. Luke 23:34. Acts 1:14, 24-25 & 4:23-30 & 7:60 & 8:22 & 10:2, 9, 30-31 & 12:5, 12 & 13:3 & 16:13, 16, 25. Rom. 12:12. Eph. 5:20 & 6:18. Phil. 4:6. Col. 4:2-3. 1 Thes. 3:10 & 5:17. 1 Tim. 2:1-3, 8 & 5:5. 2 Tim. 1:3. Heb. 13:15, 18. James 1:5-6 & 4:2-3 & 5:16-18. 1 Pet. 1:17 & 2:5 & 3:12. 1 John 3:22 & 5:14.

100. What does the preface of the Lord's prayer teach us?

The preface of the Lord's Prayer, which is, *Our Father who art in heaven,* teacheth us to draw near to God with all holy reverence and confidence, as children to a father,* able and ready to help us; and that we should pray with and for others.

*Rom. 8:15. For ye have not received the spirit of bondage again to fear; but ye have received the spirit of adoption, whereby we cry Abba, Father.

101. What do we pray for in the first petition?

In the first petition, which is, *Hallowed be thy name,* we pray that God would enable us and others to glorify him in all that, whereby he maketh himself known, and that he would dispose all things to his own glory.*

Petition, Humble request.

Hallowed, Sanctified or honored, as becomes the name of God.

*Rom. 11:36. Of him and through him, and to him are all things, to whom be glory forever. Amen.

102. What do we pray for in the second petition?

In the second petition, which is, *Thy kingdom come,* we pray that Satan's kingdom may be destroyed,* that the kingdom of grace may be advanced, ourselves and others brought into it, and kept in it, and that the kingdom of glory may be hastened.

Satan's kingdom, The dominion, or power of the devil over men.

*Ps. 68:1. Let God arise, let his enemies be scattered; let them also that hate him flee before him.

103. What do we pray for in the third petition?

In the third petition, which is, *Thy will be done on earth as it is in heaven,* we pray that God by his grace would make us able and willing to know, obey, and submit to his will in all things, as the angels do in heaven.

104. What do we ray for in the fourth petition?

In the fourth petition, which is, *Give us this day our daily bread,* we pray that of God's free gift we may receive a competent portion of the good things of this life,* and enjoy his blessing with them.

Competent portion, Sufficient share.

*Prov. 30:8. Give me neither poverty nor riches; feed me with food (allotted to) me. 1 Tim. 6:8.

105. What do we pray for in the fifth petition?

In the fifth petition, which is, *And forgive us our debts, as we forgive our debtors,* we pray that God for

Christ's sake would freely pardon all our sins,* which we are the rather encouraged to ask, because by his grace we are enabled from the heart to forgive others.+

*Ps. 51:1. Have mercy upon me, O God, according to thy loving kindness; according unto the multitude of thy tender mercies blot out my transgressions.

+Mat. 6:14. If ye forgive men their trespasses, your heavenly Father will also forgive you. Mat. 18:21-35. Mark 11:25-26. Luke 6:37 & 17:3-4. Eph. 4:32. Col. 3:13.

106. What do we pray in the sixth petition?

In the sixth petition, which is, *And lead us not into temptation, but deliver us from evil,* we pray that God would either keep us from being tempted to sin,* or support and deliver us, when we are tempted.+

Temptation, Anything that entices or persuades us to sin, or that diverts or discourages us from our duty.

*Mat. 26:41. Watch and pray, that ye enter not into temptation.

+Ps. 19:13. Keep back thy servant also from presumptuous sins; let them not have dominion over me.

107. What doth the conclusion of the Lord's prayer teach us?

The conclusion of the Lord's prayer, which is, *For thine is the kingdom, and the power, and the glory, forever, Amen,* teachest us to take our encouragement in prayer from God only,* and in our prayers to praise him, ascribing kingdom, power, and glory to him; and in testimony our desire and assurance to be heard, we say, *Amen.*

Ascribing, Acknowledging as due.

Amen, A wish and hope that it may be as we ask.

*Dan. 9:18. We do not present our supplications before thee for our righteousnesses, but for thy great mercies.

+1 Chron. 29:11. Thine, O Lord, is the greatness, and the power, and the glory, and the victory, and the majesty; for all that is in the heaven and in the earth is thine; thine is the kingdom. O Lord, and thou art exalted as head above all.

INDEX
TO THE ASSEMBLY'S CATECHISM

A considerable number of scriptures upon the following subjects are referred to. The figures placed at the right hand of the subjects denote the questions in the Assembly's Catechism, under which the references are respectively placed.

Adoption   34
Adultery 70
Atonement of Christ 25
Bearing false witness 76
Blessedness of believers 38
Coveting 79
Day of judgment 28
Decrees of God 7
Depravity of man 18
Divinity of Christ 6
Divinity of the Holy Spirit 6
Duties of children to parents 63
Election 20
Faith 85
Glorifying and enjoying God 1
Idolatry 45, 49

Knowing God 46
Murder 67
Offices of Christ 23
Perfections of God 4
Perseverance of saints 36
Prayer 99
Profanity 53
Providence of God 11
Punishment of the wicked 19
Repentance 85
Sabbath 57, 60
Stealing 73
Trinity 6
Works 90

COMMENTS FOR TEACHERS

The following recommendations and comments were included in the 1810 edition of Emerson's Evangelical Primer:

Minor Doctrinal Catechism:

This Catechism contains the leading doctrines of the Bible, expressed in a plain and connected manner. Note: It is earnestly recommended to teachers of this Primer, that they exert themselves to make learners repeat the answers distinctly, deliberately, understandingly, solemnly, and in all respects properly, as possible.

Minor Historical Catechism:

This Catechism contains an outline of scripture history, in short and easy questions and answers.

The author has long been of opinion, that the attention of young children may be directed to scripture history with great advantage. It is easily understood, very engaging, and full of instruction. Perhaps there is no way, in which moral and religious information can be conveyed to the young mind more clearly and impressively, than by interesting passages of sacred history. How often have children had their attention fixed and their minds delighted in hearing from parental lips an account of Noah, of Joseph, of Moses, of Gideon, of Samson, of Samuel, of David, of Elijah, of Daniel, of Jesus, etc. How beneficial the knowledge and impressions, that have been gained in this way.

It is necessary that children should have some acquaintance with scripture history in order to understand other parts of the Bible, to profit by sermons, which they hear, and religious books, which they read.

The business of learning the lessons of history, which God has revealed for our instruction, is so great, so interesting, and so important, that it can hardly be begun too early. As soon therefore as the child can speak intelligibly, the tender parent of affectionate friend may begin the delightful task of teaching. For those, who are very young, some of the easiest questions and answers may be selected from this Catechism. For children more than five years old it may be best in general to learn the Primer through in course.

Care must be taken however not to overstrain or burden the tender mind, lest you weaken it, or occasion a disrelish for your instructions. Ask your child a few questions at first. Encourage him, when he answers well; and cheerfully tell him, when he fails. Endeavor to make him consider your instructions a privilege, and render them as pleasing as possible. After asking him a few questions, talk about them familiarly, and relate to him the whole story, of which they may constitute a part. In order to do this with pleasure and advantage, you may often find it useful to recur to the Scriptures referred to after the answers. It may be very useful for the child to turn to these passages as soon as he is able.

The Westminster Assembly's Shorter Catechism

This excellent Catechism has stood the test of ages. It was composed in the 1640's by more than 100 ministers at Westminster in England. It is called The Shorter Catechism, to distinguish it from a larger one made by the same Assembly. WE AGREE WITH EMERSON'S CLAIM THAT it has probably done ten times more good that any volume written by man uninspired; and is undoubtedly the best Catechism in existence.

The Notes are mostly those of Dr. Watts, which have been found so useful to explain to the young learner the meaning of important words and phrases.

It is confidently hoped that this edition of the Assembly's Catechism will be found at least as valuable for children as any in print; and that young people will derive much instruction, and Christians unspeakable satisfaction from carefully consulting the numerous Scriptures referred to.